TRIANGLE
TRUE CRIME STORIES

TRIANGLE TRUE CRIME STORIES

Cathy Pickens

THE
History
PRESS

Published by The History Press
Charleston, SC
www.historypress.com

Front cover: Ivy Bluff Prison tower. *Courtesy of Robinson-Spangler Carolina Room, Charlotte Mecklenburg Library. Back cover, top*: Raleigh skyline. *Courtesy of Elijah Mears on unsplash.com, elijah-mears-SScbTSOJ00E-unsplash. Back cover, bottom*: Parking deck. *Courtesy of Jay Mantri on Pixabay.*

First published 2021

Manufactured in the United States

ISBN 9781467147453

Library of Congress Control Number: 2021934320

Notice: The information in this book is true and complete to the best of our knowledge. It is offered without guarantee on the part of the author or The History Press. The author and The History Press disclaim all liability in connection with the use of this book.

Always, for those with stories to tell…and those willing to listen.

CONTENTS

CONTENTS

ACKNOWLEDGEMENTS

A gain, this book—and so many other wonderful things in my life—wouldn't have happened without other writers, researchers, librarians, journalists and those who've investigated and preserved these stories. Special thanks to Paula Connolly, Dawn Cotter, Terry Hoover and Ann Wicker, the Really Mean Women of legend, veterans of many sessions discussing what makes a book work, and to John Jeter, who has earned his spot among the tribe. Shelia Bumgarner at the Charlotte-Mecklenburg Public Library, as always, is a wonder at locating amazing photographs. And Kate Jenkins, Jonny Foster and the amazing team at The History Press produce beautiful books to share these North Carolina stories.

INTRODUCTION

The Triangle area of North Carolina centers on the cities of Raleigh, Durham and Chapel Hill and their universities and research facilities, but the first major draw to the region was government. Oddly enough, North Carolina's original seat of government was in Charles Towne, South Carolina, until the colony was divided in 1712. Afterward, North Carolina's government sat wherever the governor lived, usually in the more populated eastern part of the state. As European settlement gradually moved inward from the coast, the seat of government moved with it.

North Carolina's capital kept up its traveling ways until the state assembly got tired of the regional rivalries and settled on a central location so that folks at either end of the long state wouldn't have to travel too far. If one had to travel to conduct state business, one would also want refreshment. According to William S. Powell's history, they decided it should "be located within ten miles of Isaac Hunter's tavern in Wake County. This had long been a popular stopping place for judges and lawyers traveling the circuit, and it was said that their decision was made because of the good rum punch served at the tavern."

Today, the region attracts those involved in state politics, those interested in the life of the mind and those interested in raising their families or retiring in a safe, beautiful place. Most people find what they come looking for, but for some, domestic tragedy, random violence and their own histories follow them here. Even in such a prosperous, diverse, modern environment, crime helps define the edges.

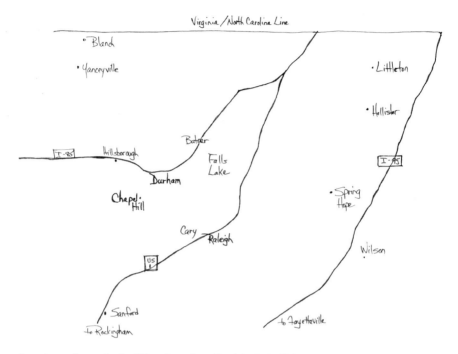

Locations of cases in the Triangle region. *Sketch by Cathy Pickens.*

These cases cover several decades of murder, fraud, family betrayal, new-tech sleuths, a suspected Cold War spy, an unsolved lover's lane murder, diligent as well as discredited investigators, a civil rights–era clash of Old South and New, the nation's largest prison escape and a couple of North Carolina's poisoners.

My family has been in the Carolinas for more than three hundred years, steeped in southern storytelling. Because any retelling of stories naturally depends on the storyteller's choices, these stories are those that, for one reason and another, captured my imagination.

This book is not a work of investigative journalism. The information is drawn solely from published or broadcast resources, including newspapers, television documentaries, appellate court cases, scholarly papers, print and online magazine articles, books and podcasts.

One of the handicaps in recounting historical events is that accounts vary. Some reported "facts" aren't accurate—or are at odds with someone else's memory or perception of the event. While I have worked to dig out as many points of view as I could find, I'm sure there are mistakes. My apologies in advance.

View down Fayetteville Street from North Carolina Capitol in Raleigh. *Photo by Elijah Mears on Unsplash.com.*

"Major," the Durham bull. *Photo by Colin Rowley on Unsplash.com.*

For me, what fascinates is not random violence but people and their lives. Some of these stories could have happened anywhere. Some made huge headlines far away from the North Carolina Piedmont. Others remain mostly in the hearts of family and friends.

All of them, woven together, demonstrate the rich variety of those who call this part of the state home, the importance of family and friends, the life shift of young people leaving home and starting their lives, the contrasts in modern cities nestled among small towns. People and their stories matter here. The stories are worth remembering, even when they involved loss and especially when they are tempered with affection and good memories.

Welcome to the Triangle region of North Carolina and its crime stories.

1
UNSOLVED

VALENTINE'S DANCE

High school sweethearts, attractive, popular, recently engaged and planning their lives together. He was an athlete voted most likely to succeed, attending North Carolina State University. She was a nursing student enrolled at Watts Hospital School of Nursing. They had a date for the Valentine's Day dance.

What could be sweeter or more romantic, especially when seen through the nostalgic haze of 1971?

But then the story morphs. Jesse McBane, nineteen, and Patricia Mann, twenty, disappear. No sign of them anywhere, even though the news media alerted people all over North Carolina. They were not the type to run away, their families said. If they wanted to hurry and get married, their families would have approved.

Then, on February 25, a surveyor found their bodies in woods just down the street from a new neighborhood. The two were tied with their backs to a tree, partially covered by leaves. They'd been dead since they'd disappeared almost two weeks earlier.

Decades passed, and the story morphs yet again. A dusty box is spotted amid a sea of old boxes in the middle of an evidence storage room, the lid off. Orange County sheriff's investigator Tim Horne couldn't help but notice the black-and-white crime scene photos lying on top.

Watts Hospital, first opened in 1895, housed the Watts School of Nursing until 1976. *Photo by Cathy Pickens.*

Almost fifty years had gone by since those photos were taken. Crime scene photos are no longer printed in black and white. Tall, handsome young men rarely sport long sideburns now. Young couples rarely have dorm curfews after a Valentine's Day dance. New technology exists—new forensic technology and new ways to broadcast the story.

For some, this story is too familiar. The family and friends of Jesse and Patricia have re-lived the details and the loss too many times. Others knew the story only as the long ago.

And someone—at least one person—knew what happened.

Was that person still alive? Would those who knew Jesse and Patricia and those who searched for answers ever know what happened? And why?

One of the new technologies brought to this case was podcasting—a new way to tell a story, a new way to reach audiences, to bring attention to a case, to spark memories, to prick consciences. Not that Tim Horne or the victims' families were wild about the podcast idea at first.

The Valentine's Day dance was held on February 12, a Friday with misting rain. Jesse picked up Patricia in the car he and his brother shared. She was

Wayside Place near where Jesse McBane's car was found parked in 1971, before the neighborhood was developed. *Photo by Cathy Pickens.*

the older of the two, by a year. He'd started in the fall at NC State University.

They left the dance, sponsored by the School of Nursing, with Patricia signed out for a later 1:00 a.m. curfew at her dormitory. They apparently drove to the Wayside cul de sac in the as-yet unbuilt subdivision of Croasdaile, about two miles away from her school. The nursing students knew the secluded wooded area and went there to spend time with their boyfriends. After all, if you lived in a dormitory in 1971 and were required to sign out for a date, you had to look for quiet places, and this was a popular lovers' lane. Ironically, a new Watts School of Nursing was later built on Croasdaile Drive, not far from the old lovers' lane.

Patricia missed her curfew. By Saturday morning, her roommates were worried. Patricia was a by-the-rules girl. She didn't miss curfew. She and Jesse weren't the kind of kids to worry their friends or their parents by just taking off.

Her friends did all the things people do when a friend isn't where she's supposed to be—they called the hospitals, called the Durham Police, called the parents, went out looking on their own.

They found Jesse's car. The car doors were locked. They could see their friends' coats on the back seat. Nothing looked out of place. There was no sign of Jesse and Patricia.

As is often the case when the missing persons are old enough to make their own decisions, the official search was slow to start. After all, a young couple can take off if they are of age. The scene showed no sign of danger or force. But as too many days passed without word, the case took on a growing sense of urgency.

Police followed leads; volunteers searched the heavily wooded area.

Twelve days later, a surveyor working about a quarter mile off a dirt road, in what would become a populated development, saw what he thought was a mannequin leg sticking out of some leaves.

He'd found their bodies. They were covered with leaves, sitting slumped against the base of a tree, hands behind them, rope around their necks.

17

The new Watts School of Nursing on Croasdaile Drive, a mile from the former lovers' lane. *Photo by Cathy Pickens.*

They hadn't been robbed. Their deaths had been violent. Patricia had been punched or kicked but not sexually assaulted. Both had been repeatedly strangled and allowed to revive. They had suffered multiple shallow knife wounds, but those were inflicted after their deaths.

The case started with several problems. A lot of time had elapsed before their bodies were found. Forensic science had smaller toolkits available in 1971. Perhaps a more difficult obstacle to overcome was garden-variety, too-common jurisdictional infighting. The crime scene was on the border between Orange and Durham Counties. Investigating agencies included the Orange County Sheriff's Office, the Durham Police Department, the State Bureau of Investigation (SBI) and the FBI. Unfortunately, the search for what happened sometimes got tangled in rivalries and an unwillingness to share information among agencies.

Later, more collaborative minds took on the case, but by then, valuable time and information was lost.

Despite missteps, some cutting-edge work was done early in the case.

In October 1971, newspapers reported that Durham detective Tim Bowers—the first detective assigned to this case—spent five hours in the New York apartment of Dr. James Brussel. Brussel, a psychologist, had gained national prominence by creating one of the first forensic psychological profiles.

In 1956, his description of the then-unknown Mad Bomber who'd terrorized New York and the electric utility Con Ed for sixteen years reportedly helped lead police to the bomber's door. George Metesky was an immigrant with an athletic build who lived with a female relative, as predicted. Brussel missed Metesky's age by ten years, and Metesky was a slob, not neat. But he normally wore a double-breasted suit, just as Brussels described, though he was wearing pajamas when police knocked on his door.

Forensic profiling isn't an exact science, but Dr. Brussel made headlines and a reputation in subsequent cases, so Detective Bowers sought him out. The two studied the crime scene photos and discussed what the investigation had uncovered during the eight months since the murders.

Brussel expected the killer would be between twenty-five and forty years old, athletic, educated, neat and precise, but not a flashy dresser. He acted alone and wouldn't be someone who took unnecessary risks. He would be familiar with the locales where the car was abandoned and where the bodies were found. Brussel saw this as a grudge killing by someone with a paranoid need to "cleanse the world."

This time, though, Brussel's description didn't lead directly to the killer's door.

A Fresh Look

In 2014, about the time Tim Horne got curious about the old box in evidence storage, Carolyn Spivey called the sheriff's office. Carolyn was Patricia's cousin, one of her closest friends and married to Jesse's best friend, David.

She'd grown up with questions the adults around her didn't always want to hear and couldn't answer, and she'd harbored those questions for forty years. She decided to call and ask some of those questions, and it was Tim Horne who took her call. He had just begun looking for the answers in that dusty box.

Horne asked the sheriff if he could reopen the cold case and then started contacting everyone he could locate who'd been involved, anyone who was still alive, including the former investigators. He shared with them what he had accumulated. Those who were still mentally able shared ideas.

Horne kept current with any technologies that might help his cases. One hope-raising possibility was a new testing method for the ropes that bound the victims. Surely, given the long period of contact with the ropes, the killer's DNA must be somewhere in those rough, thick fibers.

The technology was an M-Vac machine. Guilford County had one of the forty machines available at the time in the United States. Similar to a wet-vac, the M-Vac sprays and vacuums up a buffering solution that suspends DNA particles and captures them for analysis. According to the company's website, the M-Vac works on materials that don't normally yield DNA samples—textured, rough, porous surfaces ranging from bricks to duffle bags.

Unfortunately, in this case, the M-Vac testing of the ropes in 2018 didn't yield enough DNA for testing.

So, what do investigators know at this point? Someone apparently approached the couple at the spot where Jesse's car was parked, subdued them in some way, perhaps forced them into the trunk of a car and moved them to the more secluded area a few miles farther away and deeper in the woods.

The killer had to be familiar with the vicinity and had to know where to find his victims, where to park his car and that he wouldn't be interrupted.

A number of notable cold cases, when solved, involve someone completely unknown, someone who never blipped on the investigator's radar. Was it a random stranger, a chance encounter? Or someone Patricia worked with and knew? Patricia did, after all, seem to be the target.

Those frustrating questions remained, unanswered. What continues to draw attention to the case is how technology—and determined investigators—have pushed the story forward, starting with Tim Bowers's long-ago visit to Dr. Brussel. For Tim Horne forty years later, the M-Vac wasn't the only new technology he was willing to try. The new technology of podcasting brought the case into public view in a way unimaginable in 1971.

The Long Dance

True crime podcasts abound. Some are casual chats over wine with loose attention to the facts. Others are rehashes of case material. The best podcasts, though, pave new ground and adhere to good journalism and good storytelling. The best respect the victims, their families and the suspects. The very best work with law enforcement when possible, rather than engaging in what can become reckless vigilantism.

Eryk Pruitt and Drew Adamek are skilled storytellers. Their backgrounds included investigative journalism, novel writing, screenwriting and true crime documentary production. They thoroughly researched the case before they approached Tim Horne. They were respectful of the family. They spent years researching every angle and winning over the families and Horne with their dedication and careful attention to details.

In 2018, announcing the release of their podcast, Pruitt wrote about the long journey that brought it to life. He and Adamek culled through public records and library microfiche, following up on the smallest details. In 2016, when the two first approached Horne, he wasn't interested in working with them. Police investigators have plenty of reasons for caution when dealing with journalists. The victims' families, through a spokesperson, also "politely declined" to meet with them.

The two continued their research. Virtually nothing was available on the internet, so they worked the case the old-fashioned way, putting together the scattered pieces of a long and complicated case. In 2017, they again asked Horne for a meeting. He looked over their materials, including the name of the man their work pointed to as the prime suspect. Horne again declined to be involved in their project.

As Pruitt recounted it, "We chatted about basketball for a few minutes. He wished us luck and sent us on our way. But five minutes later, my phone rang. It was Horne.…'Let's stop kidding around,' he said. 'You've figured out the name of our primary suspect.'"

After signing formal documents and pledging confidentiality, the team set to work. The two podcasters expanded the concept for their podcast. They wanted listeners to hear the voices of those involved telling the story in their own words.

Pruitt said they were constantly reminded that investigators *never* let novices into their cases. But the two podcasters proved useful—and apparently trustworthy. "Law enforcement had always been unable to rule out three suspects," Pruitt wrote. "In exchange for access to the case file, we were given one caveat: We had to build a case against all three suspects. The goal was to not only show that one person committed these murders, but that the other two did not."

In eight episodes, *The Long Dance* used a mix of audio interviews (thanks to the contributions of sound engineer Piper Kessler) to reveal the case to listeners. They methodically unraveled the involvement of three key suspects, including a doctor who worked with Patricia at Watts Hospital. From the first, he was a person of interest who consistently refused to cooperate with police.

The podcasters didn't latch like barnacles to one suspect; they stayed open to wherever the investigative path led. The two carefully checked their three suspects' histories and reputations, their alibis, their past run-ins with the law. Two are now dead—and evidence seemed to exclude them. The third was the doctor who, in the early days of the investigation, hired a lawyer and refused to take a polygraph. He later refused to voluntarily give a DNA sample. A prime suspect in 1971, he remained one.

While the details of their investigation create an intriguing intellectual puzzle, what brought the podcast to life were the interviews. Patricia's cousin described what good kids Patricia and Jesse were. They were saving themselves for marriage—a pledge noted even in the Bible-toting small-town South fifty years ago. They were working to be financially stable and ready to start their own family.

Their kinfolk and friends were thrown akilter by their loss. Any unresolved violent death leaves scars, but outsiders are rarely exposed to what those scars feel like, through the voices of friends and family.

Without the dedication of investigator Tim Horne, the podcasters and others, this case would join a list of unsolved murders no longer being investigated. Though it remains unsolved, the victims and their families haven't been without a voice. Keeping the case in the public eye might yet yield that piece of much-needed evidence.

MISSING FAITH

Every year, thousands of college students stream into the Triangle area to one of the greatest concentrations of institutions of higher learning in the country. Those students leaving home to start their independent lives often carry with them hopes and dreams for their families as well as themselves.

For Faith Hedgepeth, from tiny Hollister, North Carolina, the eighty-mile drive to attend Chapel Hill was a world away from her close-knit family, her community and her friends. Faith, according to her mother, loved being part of her Haliwa-Saponi tribal community, participating in their powwows and events. Faith was a young woman who joyfully immersed herself in life and in those around her.

The Old Well, an iconic symbol of the University of North Carolina at Chapel Hill since 1897. *Photo by Cathy Pickens.*

She made friends easily, she was a dedicated student who earned scholarships, she aimed to be a pediatrician or a teacher, to work with children back in her community. She was active in campus life, including the Alpha Pi Omega sorority, the country's oldest Native American sorority, which was founded on the Chapel Hill campus.

In short, her story started as any parents would wish for their college-bound daughter, which made its tragic end so difficult.

On September 7, 2012, early in the fall semester at the University of North Carolina, Faith had a normal college student's day: she went to a sorority event and then spent time in the library finishing a paper until about 11:30 p.m. Before 1:00 a.m., Faith, with her roommate and friend Karena Rosario, were recorded on security footage entering the Thrill nightclub near campus.

About an hour later, her roommate felt sick and needed to go home. The cameras recorded them leaving at 2:07 a.m.

Faith took Karena back to their apartment and helped settle her in the bathroom, where Karena alternated being sick with texting or calling friends.

Faith went to the bedroom and settled in for the night.

When Karena felt better, she called a friend to come pick her up about 4:30 a.m., not ready to end the night. Later that morning, Karena needed a paper that she'd left in the apartment and wanted Faith to bring it to campus. Faith didn't answer Karena's calls. About 10:00 a.m., a friend drove Karena to the apartment to pick up her paper.

Faith's car was still in the apartment parking lot. They found her in the bedroom.

Faith had been beaten and bludgeoned, and there was a deep indentation on her forehead, apparently from an empty Bacardi Peach Red bottle found in the bedroom. Those responding to the scene saw exactly what Karena had described to the 911 operator: blood everywhere.

It was any parent's worst nightmare. A nightmare, too, for anyone who knows or works with college students anywhere. The sudden, violent, angry death of a bright, engaging life.

The Evidence

The tragedy in this case was compounded because it remained unsolved.

A week after that 911 call, on September 14, 2012, the Chapel Hill police asked a court to temporarily seal the records in the case to prevent release to the public. The autopsy results and the documents laying out the case for search warrants, they felt, held key evidence, the kind of information "known only to police, witnesses and perpetrator(s)," according to the request to seal. Police can use unusual details from a scene to check witness statements, to perhaps catch an interviewee with a detail impossible to know if the person hadn't been on the scene. They didn't want details broadcast and dissected

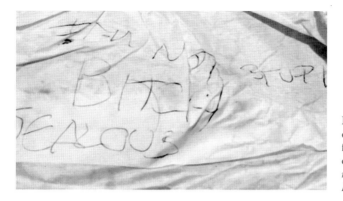

Message scrawled on white paper bag found at Hedgepeth crime scene. *Photo released by Chapel Hill Police Department.*

on news media until they had a better grasp of what happened, until they'd had ample time to investigate leads.

As the investigation continued, officials periodically renewed the requests and kept the records sealed for two years.

When released in 2014, the records revealed an unusual piece of evidence found at the scene: on the blood-soaked bed near Faith lay a plain white paper bag commonly used for food take-away. On it was scrawled in large, angry capital letters: I'M NOT STUPID BITCH JEALOUS.

Who leaves such a note? Did it prove the killer knew Faith? How, in such a blood-covered scene, had this bag stayed clean and white? What did it mean?

Another key piece of evidence was the 911 call.

From the start, to investigators who heard Karena's 911 call, her choice of words, her tone of voice, even the timing of the call raised questions. The call came in at 11:01 a.m. The dispatcher answered, "911. Where is your emergency?" Karena replied, "I just walked into my apartment and my friend is unconscious. There's blood everywhere! I don't know what happened."

The 911 dispatcher calmly asked Karena questions to determine what assistance she might give Faith before medics could arrive. When the dispatcher finally got Karena to say Faith was already cold to the touch, she told Karena to leave the room and wait for the police.

When released in 2014, the public heard the recording for the first time. Now others heard what had raised questions for the police. Each person reacts differently to stress and grief, but many found it odd that as the 911 operator asked Karena to check on Faith's condition, Karena never mentioned a friend was with her or asked her friend to help check on Faith.

A study published in the FBI *Bulletin* contrasted 911 homicide calls made by innocent people and calls made by someone later proven to be involved in the death. Certain indicators occurred more often when the caller was involved: starting with "hi" or a calm, polite tone rather than an urgent plea for help; extraneous details; repetition (to buy time to think); not responding to questions or to requests for action. These occurred more often with guilty callers.

What investigators heard in this particular 911 call raised questions—the questions they asked Karena in hours of interviews.

The Investigation

The investigation began where investigations always do—with those closest to the victim. Faith had lots of friends. The day of her murder was a typically busy day for the college student, with plenty of encounters. Faith had dated several guys, some only casual dates and some more serious. Her roommate, Karena, had an active dating life, one that intersected with Faith's life in one important instance.

Karena had an ex-boyfriend, Eriq Takoy Jones IV. Their history had not been smooth. After one incident too many, Karena changed the apartment locks. Jones had kicked in the apartment door and Karena's bedroom door and pushed her to the floor. At that point, Faith encouraged Karena to get a restraining order against Jones. The restraining order might have caused more animosity, according to friends—directed at Faith.

Jones wasn't the only man in the girls' lives, but he was a guy who had let people know he was angry with Faith for getting involved and getting between him and Karena.

The day before Faith's murder, Jones changed his Facebook photo to read: "Dear Lord, Forgive me for all of my sins and the sins I may commit today. Protect me from the girls who don't deserve me and the ones who wish me dead."

What did it mean, in light of what happened to Faith?

Friends knew about the issues between Karena, Eriq and Faith, and some were mystified when they watched television coverage of the discovery of her body. One told interviewers how surprised she was because, on the day of the murder, Eriq seemed to seek out news cameras, talking about how sweet Faith was. "Whoever did this deserves to burn," Eriq said while standing outside the crime scene tape at the apartment complex. Friends knew he didn't like Faith. He'd been very open about that.

The scene yielded unknown male DNA from a semen sample and from the bloody rum bottle. Had detectives been able to match the DNA to any men close to the case, to any of the girls' past or present boyfriends, to anyone else who might have been around the apartment, the case would already be solved. But the DNA didn't match—not Jones or anyone else in the girls' circle of friends the police tested.

Another potential piece of evidence in the case was almost erased. The morning of Faith's murder, a close friend of hers woke for class to find a voicemail from Faith, left in the wee hours of the morning. Listening to the scratchy, random sounds, the friend assumed Faith had, once again, sent a pocket-dial—something Faith's phone often did.

The friend erased the message, thinking it unimportant—until she got word that Faith was dead. She realized the call might, just might, be important. Her cell phone provider helped her figure out how to retrieve the message, and she called police. She knew this might be one of Faith's last communications.

The Chapel Hill police listened to the message but dismissed it. Nothing discernable could be heard. And the call came in at 1:23 a.m., a time when police knew exactly where Faith was—she had entered the Thrill nightclub about forty minutes earlier and wouldn't leave for another forty minutes. Security cameras clearly showed her coming and going from the club.

So, the background noise on the pocket-dial had to be from the club. It couldn't be from the time she was murdered.

Other odd bits of evidence came in as investigators peeled back the layers, trying to learn about the complex, interlaced lives of the students around Faith. After she'd turned in for the night, after the trip to the nightclub, after helping Karena home, Faith apparently sent some texts. One went to a former boyfriend; they had remained friends. Faith's text said they should get back together, which the young man found odd since they hadn't been talking lately.

Her father thought that text was odd for another reason. He described his daughter as obsessive, "almost OCD about punctuation." But this text opened with "Youre probably sleeping." Her dad knew she wouldn't send a text like that.

If she didn't, who did? And why? Was it just a late-night typing error? Or was someone else using her phone?

As the investigation progressed, some observers criticized authorities for keeping information sealed. Could a small department in a small city like Chapel Hill really handle an investigation like this? Why so secretive?

In October 2013, a year after the murder, the Chapel Hill police formally asked the State Bureau of Investigation to join the investigation. The SBI can bring a variety of lab and investigative resources and a range of experience into a homicide investigation. Some questioned the delay.

On September 5, 2014, two days shy of the second anniversary of the murder, Durham County court officials unsealed some three hundred pages of investigative documents, making available the 911 call and the search warrants. For those reporting on the case, the documents either revealed new details for the first time or confirmed rumors.

A New Investigator

In early 2016, Celisa Lehew became lead investigator on Faith's case. Lehew had worked her way up in the city of Chapel Hill Police Department, including patrol supervisor and assistant chief. She knew about handling a hot-seat investigation involving a murdered student—she had served as lead investigator in 2008 when Chapel Hill student body president Eve Carson had been murdered.

In March 2008, Carson, the studious and popular Morehead-Cain scholar, turned down an invitation to party after the Florida State basketball game; she went back to her apartment to study. Soon after 3:30 a.m., someone took her from her apartment on a quiet back street, drove her around to ATMs and shot her five times in the street, all in the early morning hours.

Thanks to enhanced ATM video and existing police records, the young killers were arrested in less than a week.

Faith's case hadn't yielded answers as quickly but not for lack of attention.

In January 2016, journalists investigating the case for *Crime Watch Daily* (now *True Crime Daily*) news program approached Arlo West, an experienced forensic audio expert. Could he clear up some of the static and enhance the voicemail message sent from Faith's phone that night?

The first issue was the time stamp on the message—had the call really been made at 1:23 a.m.?

Journalists reported the brand of phone owned by both Faith and the friend who received her voicemail message had a quirk—the time stamps on calls weren't always accurate. Voicemails were not always transmitted at the times indicated.

In another Triangle-area case, an inaccurate time stamp played a critical part in resolving the rape charges made against three Duke lacrosse players in 2006. Could this be another instance where timing was, indeed, everything? Did the garbled call take place not at the nightclub but later, when Faith was being murdered?

The message itself presented another critical question: what was said on the recording? Arlo West enhanced and studied the recording and produced a transcript of what he deciphered from the message. Some hear the words he heard; others don't.

Most who listen to it agree on one thing: more than one voice is recorded— two girls and one or maybe two guys. Her family believes they recognize the sound of Faith's voice, though not all the words spoken. And most think it sounds like an altercation of some sort.

Did an altercation happen at the nightclub? Or later, at Faith's apartment? Did the altercation lead to her murder? Or was her murder actually being recorded?

Paul Holes, a retired cold case investigator from California who continued to work on cases around the country, cohosts *The Murder Squad* podcast with journalist Billy Jensen. In discussing this case, Holes explained how subjective audio recognition can be. He suggested having other audio experts without any previous knowledge of the case enhance and review the voicemail message. Best to hear this evidence without preconceived notions, Holes said.

Cold cases fade from the public's attention. Media quit carrying the story. Even with key new evidence—the 911 call, the voicemail, the paper bag note and details from the crime scene—now in the hands of journalists, podcast investigators and citizen-sleuths, the updates got shorter, moved back farther into the newspaper, fell off the news broadcasts.

Faith's family and friends continued to hold memorials on the anniversary of her murder, inviting journalists and working to keep the story in the news. They cooperated with television documentarians and podcasters to the same end. In cold cases, someone's conscience might be pricked, seeing how much the family still longs for answers. A friend might be protecting someone—from love or fear or uncertainty. A falling out might mean that friend becomes willing to talk, given a nudge on the evening news.

In 2016, to bring new attention to the case, detectives released to the *20/20* news magazine program a likeness created by Parabon NanoLabs. Parabon is a DNA technology company working with health care firms on a number of high-tech research projects. Parabon has also pioneered new DNA technology solutions for law enforcement.

In Faith's case, Parabon took the DNA samples found at the scene and used its new DNA phenotyping technology to predict what the owner of that DNA could look like. The result is what some call a genetic mugshot.

The technology is still developmental. For instance, the composite picture created for the Golden State Killer case in California didn't resemble the

killer once he was caught. But in other cases, the results have been remarkably recognizable.

Like most traditional mugshots, the computer-generated result might not lead to a killer's identification. But it may spark enough interest to encourage the person who knows something to no longer keep quiet.

Phenotyping introduced some important new elements to this case: the killer was likely of mixed European and Latino descent (which, in the language of phenotyping, includes those of Indigenous heritage), most likely with black hair, olive skin, brown eyes and few to no freckles.

As of early 2020, police had interviewed two thousand people. Hundreds of male DNA samples have been run with no matches to the DNA found at the scene.

Faith's case isn't the only unsolved murder of a Chapel Hill coed. Longtime Tarheels know the story of Suellen Evans. In July 1965, Suellen was attending summer school classes. Her class finished at about noon, and she took her usual shortcut through the Coker Arboretum back to her dorm room in Cobb Hall.

A man attacked her in the park near the Raleigh Street exit across from McIver Hall. She fought back. He stabbed her twice, once in the neck and once in the chest through to her heart. Her last words to those who came to her rescue: "He tried to rape me…I believe I'm going to faint."

The police and the SBI went into high gear. Students helped with a sweep-search of the Arboretum. But leads petered out, and possible suspects were excluded. The case remains unsolved over five decades later.

Faith's case had a critical distinction with Suellen's case, though—DNA. As Chapel Hill police chief Chris Blue said, "This is a very strong case. What we need to do is connect that case to Faith's killer."

The case file offers plenty of evidence, including DNA—which has matched none of the men known to be connected with Faith. Was it a random attack, like Eve Carson's? An attacker taking advantage of the door Faith's roommate left unlocked early that morning? Speculation

Opposite: Sign at an entrance to the Coker Arboretum in the heart of the UNC–Chapel Hill campus. *Photo by Cathy Pickens.*

Above: Gate leading onto a shaded path in the Coker Arboretum. *Photo by Cathy Pickens.*

Above: Faith Hedgepeth's grave marker commemorating her youthful energy and her deep faith. *Photo by Cathy Pickens.*

Left: Memorials for Faith to honor her love of UNC–Chapel Hill and her favorite hot sauce. *Photo by Cathy Pickens.*

suggests more than one person might have been at the scene. But whether Faith knew him or not, nothing in the file has yet to incontrovertibly link Faith and her killer.

Meanwhile, her father, Roland Hedgepeth, keeps binders full of his own research. He knows the police are working on the case, but he, too, has worked it, made his own phone calls, asked his own questions and meticulously recorded it all. He keeps his investigative materials separate from the even larger gathering of binders recording Faith's life and her achievements. Refusing to shy away from doing what they can to keep her memory and her case before the public, Faith's family has participated in interviews, television true crime documentaries and podcasts. Someone somewhere knows what happened. Someday, someone will talk.

Her family and friends, as evidenced by the binders in her father's house, know Faith's life is much larger and more important to them than her death. They work toward solving the one while celebrating the other—a difficult balance for any victim's family and friends.

NEW FORENSICS

Elusive DNA

Since 2000, when *CSI* first aired on television, cavalier expectations have developed about what is still hard-fought legal ground. We assume investigators can get DNA and we know DNA solves crimes. End of story.

Anyone who watches television knows we can be spied on and what can be revealed by everything from our blood to our cell phone movements—and the reach of technology continues to expand. But suspects also watch television and read true crime. One Raleigh murder investigation pitted a compulsive and smart suspect against dedicated police officers in a battle of wits over how much of his secretions he could keep to himself.

Starting Her Life

When Stephanie Bennett finished Roanoke College and moved into a Raleigh apartment complex with friends, she followed the same path as many twenty-somethings—the path that brings lots of young newcomers to the Triangle area every year. Bennett left her small hometown for city lights, job opportunities and excitement and met evil instead, when her path happened to cross that of an odd, secretive stranger.

Bennett's nude body was found in May 2002 on the floor of her apartment. The path to catching her killer would be a twisted one.

Veteran Raleigh detective Lieutenant Chris Morgan's white fedora, physical presence and deep drawl made him hard to ignore. The "guy in the white hat" took murder cases personally and was the first lead detective assigned to the Bennett case. At the time the Bennett investigation began, Morgan was also working to bring research scientist Eric Miller's killer to justice for Miller's poisoning death in December 2000. (See chapter 4.)

Morgan was nearing retirement; in fact, he'd let the date pass and kept working while he pursued the poisoner. The Bennett case turned out to be the one Morgan wouldn't solve before he retired, but he'd brought in the key investigator who would continue the three-year search.

He enlisted Ken Copeland from the sex crimes unit, wanting Copeland's expertise for this sex-related homicide. Copeland's reputation as "The Garbage Man" didn't hurt; he was famous for meticulously picking through every piece of evidence, and this case needed those skills.

As the investigation began in 2002, the usual suspects, like Stephanie's boyfriend, were quickly eliminated, leaving the detectives with a real whodunit. The first clear break in the case didn't come until almost three years after the murder. In early 2005, Detective Ken "The Garbage Man" Copeland returned to the scene to get a fresh look. He began by talking to witnesses who'd seen a peeping Tom prowling the cluster of neighboring apartment complexes in 2002. From his sex crimes unit experience, Copeland knew peepers sometimes move on to more violent behavior. Those witnesses offered him some good leads.

From the DNA evidence at the scene, investigators knew the suspect was a white male. A witness at the apartment complex had seen a white male peeping into windows one night and had later seen the same guy walking a big dog, a Rottweiler.

Turns out, several attentive renters had suspected the "strange bird" with the dog who lived in an apartment complex next door to Stephanie's complex. Thanks to Detective Copeland's careful sifting of information gathered from the apartment residents, the cops finally got a name for the "strange bird" with the Rottweiler: Drew Planten.

Early in the search, the investigators knew one thing: "When we find the guy who won't give us his DNA, we've found the guy." Over the years, they'd asked a few hundred men for DNA exemplars. All had voluntarily given samples. Drew Planten was the one who refused.

The Hunt

For those who tracked him, trying to get a DNA sample became one of the craziest DNA hunts ever documented. For investigators, Planten's determination to protect his every secretion was the gauntlet thrown down.

Planten refused to voluntarily "aid police in their investigation." That was his absolute right under the U.S. Constitution. It was also the detectives' right to watch him going about his daily business so they could pick up anything he discarded. Under the law, once something has been left behind, thrown in the trash or even spit onto the pavement, the owner has no "reasonable expectation of privacy" in that water bottle, spit, cigarette butt or garbage bag full of trash.

The more the police watched Planten, the more the cat-and-mouse game intensified. His efforts to keep them from getting anything that would give them his DNA went to ludicrous extremes.

Planten never threw out any trash at his apartment complex, apparently flushing whatever he could. He never spit on the ground or discarded a drink can or water bottle, and he didn't smoke, so he left no cigarette butts.

Detectives dogged his trail, waiting for him to make a misstep. He didn't.

Finally, detectives went to Planten's work supervisor at North Carolina's Department of Agriculture lab. She liked Planten, found him a good worker.

The North Carolina Department of Agriculture Lab, Drew Planten's employer.
Photo by Cathy Pickens.

She couldn't believe he had anything to do with the murder. She prayed about what she should do and then agreed to help police get a sample, certain it would eliminate him from suspicion.

She arranged a lunch outing for the whole office to a Golden Corral restaurant. Any glass he drank from or utensils he ate with could be taken and tested. But Planten was sly. Cops seated nearby watched as Planten ate only finger food.

He tucked his napkin in his pocket rather than leave it on the table. He drank from a straw and then tucked the straw in his pocket when he went to the restroom.

He dried his hands on his pants.

Watching his caution in the restaurant, the officers hoping to snag evidence were more convinced of his guilt—who goes to such extremes otherwise? They also grew more frustrated.

Then they had a moment of elation. On the buffet sat a pan of Planten's favorite dessert—banana pudding. He couldn't resist banana pudding, but he couldn't eat it with his fingers. Was this his kryptonite?

The officers watched as he nibbled only from the end of a fork and compulsively wiped it clean. When he finished, he wiped it for five minutes. His workmates apparently were so accustomed to his idiosyncrasies that they didn't take notice.

As the group left the restaurant, Planten suddenly turned and disappeared back inside. His supervisor worried he'd caught on to the police presence. He'd simply slipped into the restaurant, where an officer watched him flush his napkin and straw down the toilet.

The officers had, however, snagged his fork off the table for testing. Had anything survived his scrupulous wiping?

Not much, as it turned out. The lab found a few DNA markers (and the DNA of a woman who'd eaten off the fork earlier, the result of a dishwasher not doing his job), but they didn't have enough for a clear match.

Detective Copeland stayed in email contact with Drew's supervisor. She began to monitor his computer work area. He was meticulous about keeping it policed, even picking loose hairs from the seat back.

In her emails, she, too, was beginning to express doubts because of his hyper-vigilance.

State Bureau of Investigation agent Mark Boodee, responsible for analyzing DNA samples, insisted Planten's workspace at the state's fertilizer lab would be the best option for getting a sample. Planten's supervisor agreed to help. Two detectives and two SBI agents waited in the car for Planten to leave work on October 17, 2005. They swabbed his computer, his desk and everything at his workstation. They found no hairs on his chair or around his desk. They took his plastic work gloves—similar to dishwashing gloves—and left a substitute pair, hoping he wouldn't notice.

Agent Boodee knew the gloves were the key. But the detectives, SBI agents and prosecutor debated among themselves about the legality of seizing the gloves without a search warrant.

Legal Protections

The U.S. Constitution protects citizens from unreasonable searches and seizures. It keeps the government at bay and doesn't force people to incriminate themselves or allow searches of person or property unless the police can prove to a judge probable cause that the target committed a crime. Probable cause strikes a balance between protecting personal privacy and allowing government intrusion to safeguard society from wrongdoing.

The Fourth Amendment protection against unreasonable search and seizure takes into account a "reasonable expectation" of privacy. But what is a reasonable expectation? That depends on where the search is conducted. Citizens have a high expectation of privacy for their person or their homes. Police can't break down the door to a house and pillage around without a search warrant or consent.

A car offers less expectation of privacy. After all, it rolls around on the streets, its glass windows showing what is plainly visible inside. If contraband (say, a fully automatic weapon) is openly visible on the front seat and an officer sees it, the car's driver can't fuss about being stopped and searched.

Court cases have argued whether law enforcement planes can fly over land to spot any illegal crops (they can) or whether they can tap a telephone or use directional microphones in vans parked on the streets to listen into gangster conversations (they can't) or whether they can attach a GPS device to a car without a warrant (they can't) or whether they can ask a driver to blow into a breathalyzer or risk losing her license (they can). The latest fights are over access to data on smartphones and whether third parties (like Apple and others) can be required to turn it over (they can, with a valid search warrant) or can be required to create software to unlock encryption (so far, no). In other words, where personal rights end and where the government's need to protect us from those who would do us harm begins is a continuing legal battleground.

Drew Planten's workstation was yet another arena of privacy issues. He worked at a state-owned facility, so the space technically belonged to the state of North Carolina. Planten's consent wasn't required to search it. In fact, as a rule, employees have no expectation of privacy in equipment (such as desks, computers, voicemail systems and the like) owned by their employers, even if the employer is a private company.

But investigators didn't want to make a mistake in gathering what could be critical evidence. They wanted to make sure that if the samples matched, the evidence would be admissible at trial.

In the end, after carefully weighing the legalities, the decision was made. The investigators nabbed the gloves—and found the DNA match to the scene of Stephanie Bennett's murder.

The DNA match allowed a search warrant for Planten's apartment. Detectives got another surprise. In addition to finding Stephanie's missing laundry basket, they also found nine handguns, forty knives, a machete and hundreds of video games. They found a videotape of a former neighbor from the apartment complex, apparently taken at a party with her friends. When they located the young woman living in Hickory, she said she still had the videotape; Planten had apparently gotten into her apartment, stolen the video, copied it and returned it. The reason was anybody's guess.

Most surprisingly, investigators linked items found in Planten's apartment—old bills addressed to a woman and one of his .45-caliber handguns—to an unsolved 1999 shooting death of a young woman in Lansing, Michigan. Planten lived there and attended Michigan State University before moving to Raleigh to take his lab job.

In October 2005, the Fugitive Task Force was called out to capture Planten. After he finished work that day, Planten walked his bicycle from the lab building toward the street. Officers chose that as the safest place to approach him.

His supervisor was standing at the building door. The sound of his bike hitting the pavement and the image of him on the ground, his hair covering his face, guns pointing at him, is a memory she said wouldn't leave her. WRAL news reporter Amanda Lamb described the supervisor's reaction: "It was a bittersweet moment, one of justice, but at the same time, one of loss, *her* loss. She lost the person she had come to believe Planten was—a meek, sensitive introvert who just wanted everyone to leave him alone."

That day, the task force officers didn't know who they were arresting until they heard Detective Copeland say, "Drew, you are under arrest for the murder of Stephanie Bennett."

Planten was held in the Wake County Detention Center before his pretrial transfer to Central Prison. *Photo by Cathy Pickens.*

The officers stood in the street and cheered.

Soon, the TV news coverage of Planten's first court appearance was played and replayed. He needed a wheelchair to carry him into the courtroom because he refused to walk. He refused to respond. He slumped forward, his long, tangled hair hiding his face. He kept his eyes closed, as if in a catatonic state. A family member later said Planten, as a child, reacted in the same way when upset with his mother.

He didn't cooperate when police tried to question him, and he didn't participate in his first court appearance.

Planten was transferred from the Wake County Jail when he refused to eat or cooperate with jailers. While held at Central Prison, Planten committed suicide. He never spoke with investigators about the crimes.

Those who loved and missed Stephanie Bennett likely cheered the extreme efforts of Raleigh police to collect the evidence to arrest Planten. They might have wished it could've happened faster or easier, but rushing to gather evidence could have shifted the line protecting our privacy too much in the wrong direction. A tough balance—what if delays left future victims at risk?

Stephanie was one of many young women who come to Raleigh and other cities to start their lives. Even the cops not actively investigating her case felt the personal burden of her unsolved murder and shared a sense of relief. Amanda Lamb said, in a documentary interview, she couldn't remember a case that concerned the community as much as this one.

Years later, on an online football forum, Drew Planten's brother acknowledged his relationship to Drew. "When ever someone Googles my name his crimes come up. I just have to accept it." He answered questions from the online community and, when asked, said it did help to discuss it with people. In a case where no answers came from the killer, those who knew Planten and knew his victims were left with plenty of questions and their own losses. In a case where pure science played a critical role, relationships proved the most enduring part of the story.

Facebook Sleuths

DNA was first introduced into a criminal investigation in 1986 in England—and rather than convict the prime suspect, it exonerated him. Since then, improvements in the technology of retrieving and analyzing DNA continue to solve cases—and free suspects—at an accelerating pace. But DNA is not the only recent crime-fighting advance in technology.

Social media has also changed the face of crime detection, also at an accelerating pace. The new technologies might be better described as a return to Agatha Christie, Dorothy L. Sayers and the Golden Age of mystery fiction. After all, Miss Marple solved cases over her knitting because she was intimately familiar with her little community in St. Mary Mead. Today, the online community is far-flung yet still oddly village-like and intimate.

Some deride the number of regular folks at home with their high-speed internet access playing citizen-sleuth or do-it-yourself detective. But even those in law enforcement acknowledge the successes and support offered by the crowdsourcing of crime investigation.

North Carolina and its high-tech Research Triangle region have not been left out in the innovations of social media detecting.

In 2004—coincidentally the same year Facebook launched—twenty-nine-year-old Deborah Deans disappeared in Spring Hope, North Carolina, east of Raleigh. With two of her four children (a five-year-old and an infant), she was living with her sister-in-law, Kimberly Hancock. According to Hancock, someone came and picked up Deborah and they left, leaving her children at the house. She never came back.

In 2013, a woman (who preferred not to be named) launched a Facebook page to alert her neighbors to local missing persons, to post photos and wanted posters and to funnel anonymous tips to law enforcement. Surely, she dreamed of helping to crack a big case—but a fifteen-year-old missing person case? That would be a tough one.

On October 20, 2019, she posted a reminder to the sixty-three thousand followers of the Fighting Crime Facebook page about the mother missing since January 2004. When Deans disappeared, she had recently moved in with her sister-in-law after serving time for passing bad checks.

An anonymous tip responded to that Fighting Crime Facebook post with detailed information about what happened to Deborah Deans. The Facebook page administrator wouldn't share details with reporters at the time the story broke—but yellow crime scene tape soon surrounded trees

A sign pointing visitors to the heart of small-town Spring Hope, North Carolina. *Photo by Cathy Pickens.*

behind Kimberly Hancock's house. A covered gurney removed from the woods put neighbors on alert.

Police had spent a few days checking out the information from the Facebook tip before obtaining a search warrant. A neighbor told WRAL reporter Adam Owens that Kimberly Hancock left her house on Wiley Road in Nash County "and as soon as she left, they went digging in the yard trying to find where someone was buried at."

When the Nash County sheriff's investigators found the shallow grave and the same wrappings described in the Facebook tip, they backed off and called for a forensic pathologist to supervise the excavation.

Investigators questioned Kimberly Hancock for several hours and then charged her with first-degree murder. The case took fifteen years to reach that point but moved quickly as soon as they located the body.

Interesting details about the accused killer's background soon surfaced.

In 1989, Kimberly Hancock, formerly Privette, had been convicted of manslaughter. She shot her father in the face as he lay on the couch. She was eighteen at the time, and her defense argued her actions were mitigated by her father's abuse. She got a six-year suspended sentence.

Even though current procedures don't provide for bail in first-degree murder cases, in May 2020, the judge applied the bail procedures in effect at the time of Deans' disappearance and murder and set bail at $750,000. However, Hancock failed to post bond and remained in jail.

In another related—and also unresolved—case, Hancock's brother, Roger Wade Ayscue, disappeared in 2009 from the nearby town of Castalia.

DEDICATED DETECTIVES

While dazzling new forensics techniques help solve crimes, techniques are useless without investigators dedicated to bringing every possible resource to bear on a case.

For twenty years, several detectives pushed to identify a child's body, found dumped underneath a billboard on Interstate 85-40 near Mebane. One of those diligent detectives was Orange County sheriff's investigator Tim Horne, no stranger to nudging a case to the cutting edges of forensic possibilities. (At the time, he was also investigating the Mann/McBane case, see chapter 1.) Horne worked on the billboard case from the beginning, even delaying his retirement trying to identify the boy so they could find his killer.

When a man mowing the verge along I-85 spotted the bones in September 1998, investigators could only surmise they belonged to a boy because of what remained of his clothes. With only skeletal remains, they could tell he was between eight and thirteen years old, too young to identify gender using only bones. His name, where he came from, how he got there—those were all mysteries.

The autopsy showed the child probably died from strangulation and probably in July, a couple of months before he was found.

The other investigator as committed as Tim Horne to finding a name for the little body was Clyde Gibbs, a medical examiner specialist with the North Carolina Office of the Chief Medical Examiner. In a 2016 interview with Steve Crump at Charlotte's WBTV, Gibbs said his job wasn't so much "who did it" but "who it is." Gibbs highlighted this case, among the other 115 unidentified remains his office was also trying to identify. A little boy found where a little boy should never have been, dumped under a billboard on the side of the interstate near Buckhorn Road, created a mystery that needed to be solved. Investigators used every means at their disposal, from talking to media to get the story out to consulting with experts.

The boy matched no child in the database at the National Center for Missing and Exploited Children (NCMEC), so he likely had never been reported missing.

Other Experts

Investigators at the North Carolina Medical Examiner's Office and the sheriff's office periodically revisited the file and retested the evidence—the bones and teeth, the insects recovered with the bones, whatever they thought might offer a thread they could pull to unravel the mystery.

They enlisted Douglas Ubelaker at the Smithsonian Institution. He used the skull to create a drawing of what the little boy might have looked like. When no one responded after the drawing was made public, Horne approached sculptor Frank Bender to sculpt a bust of the child.

Bender became nationally known for his 1989 work in creating an age-progressed bust of John List, a fugitive for eighteen years. List murdered his wife, his mother and his three children in New Jersey before he disappeared. Bender started with photos almost twenty years old. He worked with forensic psychologist Richard Walter, whose profile of List suggested the kind of heavy-framed glasses he would likely be wearing.

The bust was shown on the television show *America's Most Wanted*, and a tip led to his capture in Denver less than two weeks later. The resemblance between the bust Bender created and the man who was hauled into court was astonishing, especially the eyeglasses.

Bender and Walter were founding members of the Vidocq Society in Philadelphia, a group of law enforcement and forensics experts who meet to hear presentations on cold cases. Michael Capuzzo's book, *The Murder Room*, paints an interesting portrait of the founders and some of the Vidocq Society cases.

The Boy Under the Billboard would be Frank Bender's last cold case. In 2010, even as he lived his last months with terminal cancer, Bender worked to create a likeness of the little boy, using standard measures for skin thicknesses and the traits discernible from the skull. As with Bender's other forensic sculptures, the face that emerged was part science, part art.

Police shared images of Bender's sculpture, hoping someone would recognize the boy and give him a name. Without a name, they had no chance of learning who had killed him.

Still, no one stepped forward and said they recognized him, even though the photos had national and international coverage.

Forensic technology continued its futuristic leaps. In 2018, Tim Horne contacted retired New Zealand lawyer Barbara Rae-Venter, who had helped crack the Golden State Killer case, the most high-profile use at the time of a new field called genetic genealogy. DNA genealogy research websites give users the ability to research ancestors or find lost family members. Typically, locating ancestors involves working up through a family tree, starting with a known person.

A small, pioneering assortment of genealogists developed techniques for using a DNA sample taken from an unknown person and working through related family trees to discover the family member who most likely contributed that unidentified sample. Genetic genealogists combine information available from DNA testing with genealogy research skills, examining census records, birth records and even modern social media accounts to work their magic.

Horne had tried every other forensic magic trick he could think of. This was worth a try.

Barbara Rae-Ventner, using the child's DNA, found he was a child of Asian and white parents. She also found, in the genealogy databases, that the child possibly had a first cousin living in Hawaii.

A phone conversation with a family member in Hawaii gave Horne what he wanted: a name. Robert Adam Whitt, called Bobby, was ten years old when he was last seen. Bobby's father told family that Bobby's mother, Myoung Hwa Cho, took him with her when she returned to her native South Korea in 1998, so no one reported him missing.

That information connected little Bobby with yet another mystery. In May 1998, two months before Bobby was killed and four months before his body was found, a woman's body had been found in Spartanburg County, South Carolina, along a road parallel to I-85. The two dump sites were about three hours and two hundred miles apart.

Myoung Hwa Cho was unidentified until her son's body had a name. Her wrists had been bound at some point. She'd been strangled.

Once they knew her name, investigators found her family. They last saw her in Concord, North Carolina, in May 1998, around the time Bobby's father, John Russell Whitt, had taken up with a new girlfriend. Bobby was living with his father and the girlfriend for a couple of months, but the girlfriend wanted to send Bobby to join his mother in South Korea. Bobby's dad, of course, knew that wasn't possible. Family members had wondered why Cho had stopped contact with everyone stateside. Her family in Korea assumed she'd just fallen out of touch. Only Whitt knew why.

When police went looking for him, Whitt was easy to locate. He was in Kentucky serving a lengthy federal prison sentence for robbing ATM users with a weapon. In May 2019, he was indicted in North Carolina on a first-degree murder charge, exactly twenty-one years after Cho was last seen in Concord.

The pieces of the story were scattered over two states, two countries and two decades. The public first heard the pieces come together when Anna Orr, Orange County assistant district attorney, laid out the story after Whitt's sentencing hearing in August 2019. Whitt pleaded guilty to both murders as second-degree offenses. He was transferred to the federal prison in Butner, North Carolina, and will serve his federal prison term for robbery until January 2037, when he will become a resident of one of North Carolina's state prisons to serve his sentence of fifty-two to sixty-four years.

Tim Horne told an ABC11 television reporter he'd kept the file on unidentified little Bobby under his desk for all those years. "Every time I turned, it hit my leg. I did this so the little boy couldn't be forgotten." Without Horne and Clyde Gibbs and others and their willingness to chase every new forensic lead, neither mother nor son would have been identified and returned to their family—and their killer would have lived his life, as he had for twenty years.

3

BAD SCIENCE

Remarkable advances in forensic science explain at least some of the recent fascination with crime stories. Cases unsolved for decades are closed thanks to the ability to test ever-smaller samples of DNA (even samples left only by touch), to test mixed samples and separate the different DNAs of victim and perpetrator and, most recently, investigative genetic genealogy's ability to identify a person not only from their own DNA but also from the DNA of family members.

The underlying premise of forensic science—which means "science for the court"—is that it should, first, be scientific: objective, unbiased and interested only in discovering, as far as possible, the truth of a matter. The results should be reproducible by other experts, and a forensic expert should testify in the same way, whether hired by prosecutor or defense.

But what if the expert is a charlatan? What if the expert has an agenda to help one side, no matter what the evidence says? Worse yet, what if a rogue expert works for the state and believes his job is to bolster the prosecution's case? What if the expert gives himself permission to put his finger on the scales of justice, allows himself to hide evidence, mislead, alter and even fabricate?

What if the expert is anything but scientific and unbiased? What if the expert lies?

Through a series of highly publicized cases, North Carolina became a poster child for bad forensic practice, even as abuses were found in other state crime labs and at the FBI.

News reports often focus on the damage done to those wrongly imprisoned, sometimes for decades. But the stories should also point to another alarming result—if the wrong person was jailed, where is the real killer?

CASES SOLVED...?

The first distant rumble of the avalanche that overtook North Carolina's State Bureau of Investigation (SBI) crime lab started when Gregory Taylor got his Nissan Pathfinder stuck in the mud. On September 26, 1991, Taylor and a friend pulled off a road near Raleigh to smoke some crack and couldn't get the truck unstuck. They walked to town that night.

Investigators were parked along the road when Taylor and his friend returned the next day.

Just a football field's length from Taylor's truck lay the body of Jacquetta Thomas, stabbed and bludgeoned to death.

Both men were arrested, though charges against Taylor's friend were later dropped.

A witness told police she'd seen Thomas with Taylor. Later, she admitted she had gotten a deal from the prosecutor for her testimony and the woman she saw wasn't Thomas. A jailhouse informant added to the "evidence" against Taylor but also proved unreliable.

What decisively slammed the cell door on Greg Taylor came from SBI agent Duane Deaver, who testified he performed a chemical test that showed the presence of blood on Taylor's truck.

With that incontrovertible forensic evidence, the jury found Greg Taylor guilty.

With his appeals of his life sentence exhausted, Taylor's future turned on an odd happenstance: another man being interviewed in another wrongful conviction case broke down and confessed to Jacquetta Thomas's murder.

Only later was it clear that the man whose confession jumpstarted Taylor's innocence inquiry had a history of confessing to other crimes—seventy, at one count. By that time, though, that man's statement had turned a spotlight on the real problems in the state's case against Taylor.

After work by attorney Christine Mumma and the Center on Actual Innocence, Taylor's case became the first heard by North Carolina's landmark Innocence Inquiry Commission—the first official body in the United States created to hear innocence claims.

In the hearing, Duane Deaver admitted that the state lab did follow-up testing on the samples from Taylor's truck. What the initial test indicated was blood simply wasn't blood. Deaver admitted that the SBI didn't share those results with the prosecution or the defense. The attorneys and the jury never heard that the most damning physical evidence against Greg Taylor was a lie.

Even more disturbing was Deaver's admission that the SBI routinely withheld exculpatory evidence—evidence that might prove a defendant's innocence. Withholding evidence that helped the defense, Deaver admitted, was SBI policy.

Greg Taylor's hearing revealed his wasn't the only case in which the SBI failed to release evidence that would help a defense attorney. It was not the only case where state analysts would testify using incomplete or misleading results. The news stunned some but only confirmed what plenty of others had long suspected.

The commission declared Greg Taylor innocent, and the governor pardoned him in 2010. To compensate for the seventeen years he spent locked away, the state paid him $750,000. He also sued the SBI agents for wrongful imprisonment and was awarded over $4.6 million. The restitution was nice, but as he pointed out in an interview, money didn't allow him to roll back time and attend his daughter's graduations or walk her down the aisle at her wedding.

Not Just Blood Evidence

The SBI's problems spread beyond the blood evidence and biology section of the lab. In one case, the analysis by a firearms examiner was so poor that another expert, a former FBI chief metallurgist, wondered if she'd even looked at the evidence.

In another case, the 1993 murder case against Floyd Brown, an SBI investigator produced a confession he claimed he'd written verbatim from Brown's statement, even though everyone who had worked with Brown knew he couldn't possibly have made such a comprehensive statement—or done the actions described in the beating death of a retired schoolteacher.

Floyd Brown's arrest for murder raised alarms with those who knew Brown as a simple, gentle man with a big smile who hung around and helped out at the Anson County Courthouse. When he was sent for evaluation to determine his mental fitness to stand trial, those who cared for him at the Dorothea Dix Hospital soon had their own doubts about his involvement.

The SBI detective violated what would today be standard practice in questioning Brown, writing out for him a confession that Brown lacked the vocabulary or verbal skill to dictate for himself. Brown, with an IQ of fifty and the mental development of a first grader, was never judged to have the capacity to go to trial, so he spent fourteen years locked away in the psychiatric hospital.

Brown was finally released in 2009 by Judge Orlando Hudson, who ruled the confession alone wasn't enough to prove Brown murdered the schoolteacher; no other evidence existed. Brown received almost $8 million in compensation from the state and a separate settlement from Anson County for the actions of sheriff's deputies in investigating the case; the judge sealed the amount the county agreed to pay.

In 2013, Brown could now afford to live with a caretaker and loved eating at Burger King, cleaning house and being driven around in his used BMW 525. He couldn't drive but liked to sit behind the wheel of the parked car. But he'd lost fourteen years of freedom.

More Questionable Evidence

In the period between Greg Taylor's conviction and his exoneration, a 2007 case involving a dentist, a horse farm and a seven-foot spear provided another glimpse into Duane Deaver, his lab section and forensic science gone wrong.

On September 12, 2007, Dr. Kirk Turner went with Greg Smithson, a family friend, to pick up some equipment from the family's horse farm. Smithson had called Jennifer Turner first to make sure she was OK with Kirk coming onto the property where she lived. The Turners were in the midst of a divorce, one made contentious by feelings bruised by infidelity and a lot of money at stake.

Kirk Turner had moved out, after twenty-three years of marriage, two weeks after starting an affair. He felt his wife's attentions had turned more to her horses and away from him over the years.

In return, Jennifer was suing Kirk's girlfriend, using a North Carolina heart balm lawsuit (see chapter 8) to recover for the loss of her husband's affections.

But when Smithson asked, Jennifer Turner said it was fine if Kirk came with him that day.

According to prosecutor Greg Brown's theory of the case, Dr. Turner came to the house that night "itching for a fight." Dr. Turner wanted his wife to drop the lawsuit against his girlfriend, a woman who'd been the family's personal banker for years.

To force her hand, Turner brought two documents for his wife: an order his attorney would file with the court to sell their thirty-five-acre farm and an affidavit from her first husband telling how her obsessive love of horses had damaged their marriage. Turner's attorney said he didn't think that would enrage her—but it did.

In an interview for *48 Hours Mystery*, Greg Smithson said he left the two of them alone in the shop building when their conversation turned to sex and reconciliation. He was uncomfortable with the personal talk and gave them some privacy.

According to Turner, his wife became quite upset as they talked together. He wanted to push things toward a settlement. Going to court in a divorce case usually benefits the lawyers more than the couple. The assets were sizable: a ten-thousand-square-foot house, the $30,000 per month support payments the court had ordered for Jennifer, the horse farm, his collections of guns and vintage Corvettes. He saw benefit in them agreeing rather than fighting.

No one other than the Turners witnessed what happened in that shed. Smithson was outside, not close enough to hear what they were saying. He testified at trial that they were only alone in the shed for two or three minutes before he heard Kirk Turner "just screaming." When Smithson rushed inside, he saw Kirk bleeding. Jennifer lay on the floor covered in blood. Kirk kept saying she'd attacked him.

Smithson tried to perform CPR on Jennifer, guided by a 911 operator, but the attempt was futile.

At his 2009 murder trial, Kirk Turner took the stand in his defense, a rare move for a defendant. After all, the state has the burden of proving its case. A defendant is presumed innocent. But in this case, the jury would need to hear what happened inside that shed out of sight of anyone else.

Only Kirk Turner was alive to tell the story.

Turner said his wife became enraged over his threat to sell her beloved horse farm. He'd also shown her that affidavit from her former husband, letting her know he would play hardball if she pushed the case into court.

Jennifer wasn't a waif of a woman; she stood five foot eleven and was used to putting in twelve-hour days working on the farm. She grabbed a decorative seven-foot spear leaning against the wall. Before he knew what happened, Turner said, she stabbed him in the leg.

Turner, like lots of men in the South, carried a pocketknife. On a reflex, he pulled it from his pocket and sliced out in her direction to ward her off. She was nearly decapitated. He was stabbed twice through the leg with the spear.

She died at the scene. He required a blood transfusion at the hospital.

Prosecutor Rob Taylor argued that Kirk Turner stabbed himself to stage the scene, to make it look as though he'd been attacked. The wounds on his thigh were clean and straight through—no twisting or wobbling. This is hard to do when dodging a spear, the attorneys argued.

Defense attorney Joseph Cheshire, a renowned Raleigh criminal defense lawyer, told CBS News correspondent Peter Van Sant that it was ludicrous to think Turner could stab himself twice. "I've had doctors say to me, 'If you were wild and crazed on PCP, maybe you could do it once, but you could never do it twice.'"

In trying to understand the scene, the jury heard from family friend Greg Smithson and from blood pattern experts.

The prosecution tried to show that Smithson was involved in the coverup of a murder. They suggested Turner's footprints in partially dried blood showed the timeline was not just a handful of minutes, that Smithson must have been helping stage the scene. They believe ninety minutes were unaccounted for, plenty of time to arrange a story. And prosecutor Brown didn't believe Smithson gave Jennifer chest compressions in an attempt to revive her.

Smithson's response, when Van Sant asked him about the doubt the prosecution tried to plant, was simple and straightforward: "I don't care too much for the prosecution in this case. I know what I tried to do."

Smithson brought something intangible into the witness box at trial. In the *48 Hours* interview, Joseph Cheshire said of Smithson, "He's what we describe down here in the South as just a good old beer drinking boy." When some jurors agreed to be interviewed after the trial, they concurred. Smithson came across as a stand-up guy, and they believed him. Simple as that.

In trials where forensic evidence is available, it often wins the day. In this case, the prosecution called in the big guns—a blood pattern analyst from the SBI's crime lab. He testified that blood found on the side of a worktable showed Jennifer was inches from the floor, not standing, when her carotid artery was cut. If she'd been standing, he said, the blood should have landed on top of the table.

The SBI also analyzed bloody footprints, suggesting Jennifer's blood had to be at least partially dried before Kirk's blood began dropping onto it.

Scientific evidence is typically given much credence by jurors, especially when it comes from an analyst at a state crime lab. A witness like that comes in carrying a lot of credibility.

But the defense had a blood pattern expert of its own: Marilyn Miller, one of the coauthors of *Henry Lee's Crime Scene Handbook* and a veteran expert witness in hundreds of trials in multiple states. She examined the inside pocket of Kirk Turner's jeans, the pocket he reached in to grab his knife to protect himself after his wife stabbed him.

The only blood and DNA inside his pocket were his own, Miller reported.

Brad Bannon, one of Kirk Turner's defense attorneys, said that proved he was stabbed and bleeding before he went for his knife, before he struck out at Jennifer Turner.

The jury deliberated six hours before finding Kirk Turner not guilty by reason of self-defense.

The jurors interviewed after the trial said the blood inside Kirk Turner's pocket convinced them he'd already been attacked, despite the evidence from the state's witness about blood spurt and height and drying blood and drops of blood.

At least one juror didn't take kindly to the media's reaction to their verdict, the implication that "we were a bunch of dumb country bumpkins that were fooled by the big, flashy lawyers from out of town. That was not the case at all. I heard the evidence in the courtroom and went with what we were shown."

Kirk Turner wasn't finished fighting. In 2011, he filed a lawsuit against SBI agents and policymakers, individually or in their official capacity, for fabricating evidence and framing him in the murder of his wife. In particular, the suit claimed the actions of Duane Deaver and his protégé, Gerald Thomas, were designed to bolster the prosecutor's version of the crime rather than to objectively analyze and present evidence of the scene.

Whether he could legally sue the state agents had to be argued before the state's supreme court. The court said the state had probable cause, based on other evidence, to indict Turner, so he couldn't sue for malicious prosecution, but it allowed the case to proceed against Deaver and Thomas. Turner could sue them for intentional infliction of emotional distress—a civil action that, if a jury agreed, could lead to punitive damages. Punitive damages aren't limited to actual loss or injury; punitive damages are designed to punish the wrongdoer.

Court records said Thomas arrived at the scene two days after the murder to analyze the blood spatter. Thomas's initial report said the bloodstain on

North Carolina Supreme Court building in Raleigh, where the appeal in Turner case was heard. *Photo courtesy of the North Carolina Judicial Branch.*

Turner's gray T-shirt "was consistent with" a bloody hand wiped on the shirt and with blood dripping onto the shirt.

Turner, in his lawsuit, contended a January 2008 meeting between a sheriff's investigator, a district attorney and Deaver worked out a theory of the case in which Turner killed his wife to avoid a costly divorce. The prosecution needed evidence to support that. They argued a bloody print on Kirk Turner's T-shirt wasn't from a bloody hand but, instead, the image of a knife wiped along the shirt, which supported the prosecution.

Deaver and Thomas worked together filming their attempts to duplicate the blood smear. Audio on the recording captured Deaver sounding like a coach or a movie director celebrating a shot. After a successful attempt, he said, "Oh, even better! Holy cow, that was a good one!" and "Beautiful! That's a wrap, baby!"

After those filmed tests, Thomas altered his written report from "bloody hand" to "pointed object." Thomas's report also said the sheriff's investigator told him he'd taken the gray T-shirt in the hospital and put it in a secure place, spread out to dry. But that investigator testified he hadn't been at the hospital—and crime scene photos show the T-shirt "crumpled on the floor, inside out" in the shop building where EMTs left it, not spread out at the hospital.

Turner's expert said the stain on the shirt was likely a mirror image smear created when emergency technicians working at the scene folded the shirt to cut it off Turner.

The state supreme court's lengthy opinion dug deeply into the law's stance on allowing suits against law enforcement agents acting in the line of duty. In this case, the court said this lawsuit could be heard by a jury. In 2018, the parties settled for $200,000.

Aftershocks

Even one allegation about deceptive state experts is serious. Whenever scientific testimony is introduced to a jury, an expert witness must explain the science and offer an expert opinion. Regular folks on juries can listen to witnesses about whether a light was red when a truck ran through it and decide what they believe happened. That's common knowledge. But a layperson can't necessarily weigh the believability of complex scientific evidence or of an expert's testimony without the help of other experts. Sometimes those "battling experts," hired by either side, have different opinions about what the evidence shows. After all, that's the job of opposing counsel—to put the other side's evidence to the test, to hold its experts to the fire to burn away the dross.

Jurors then decide which is most credible.

In 2009, almost two decades after Greg Taylor's arrest based on Duane Deaver's faked blood evidence, Kirk Turner was acquitted. That same year, Floyd Brown—arrested on a "confession" he wasn't capable of giving—was released.

The number of questionable convictions over such a stretch of time illustrates the great weight jurors—and judges—give scientific experts, especially those wearing the imprimatur of the state lab.

Such abuses weren't just happening in North Carolina. Also in 2009, two national reports focused on crime labs and criminal cases across the country.

Law professors—including one professor involved in introducing DNA evidence at O.J. Simpson's trial—studied cases of those freed after wrongful convictions thanks to better DNA testing. The conclusions were alarming. In 60 percent of the cases, the state's experts misstated the evidence. Those weren't isolated or scattered outcomes—of the 156 freed defendants, bad evidence was found in 82 cases and came from 52 labs or hospitals in 25 different states.

The convicted had all been exonerated thanks to DNA testing, but at their initial trials, forensic evidence also played a critical role in convicting them. The experts at the first trials testified mostly about biological (blood and semen) and hair comparison evidence; some of the cases included bite marks, shoe prints, fibers and fingerprints as well as DNA evidence. All had led to wrongful convictions.

The study cited the lack of clear scientific standards (such as how many points are required to declare a "match"), lack of requirements that new techniques be validated by scientific peers to eliminate "junk science" and lack of oversight for testing labs as common causes for sending the wrong person to prison—and letting the real criminal go free.

Our adversarial legal system assumes the opposing side can refute the bad experts with experts of their own, but that assumption failed in these cases. Attorneys for indigent defendants can request funds to hire defense experts, but not all requests are granted. And not all attorneys are prepared to dismantle and debunk bad science on cross-examination.

In summary, the professors' study said, "the invalid science testimony described here ranges from cases in the 1980s involving conventional forensic disciplines employing visual comparison, to serology analysis employing clear population statistics, to the use of modern DNA technology in the 1990s. Though the technology has changed over time, the sources of human error, misinterpretation, and misconduct have not."

Another 2009 report, this one by the National Academies of Science, recommended separating crime labs from law enforcement agencies, that crime labs should be independent and not be a branch of an investigative unit. Labs should be evaluated, analysts' work regularly observed and standards set. Some of what passes for common knowledge (such as the uniqueness of fingerprints and the number of shared identifiers needed) has not been subjected to peer-reviewed scientific research. Science should be science-based, objective and able to be duplicated by other unbiased scientists.

Back in North Carolina, the rumbles of an avalanche began only with whispers and raised eyebrows and quiet conversations between defense attorneys and experts they hired to evaluate and perhaps refute the state's evidence.

But in August 2010, the rumbles became public. Raleigh's *News & Observer* ran a four-part series on "Agents' Secrets," laying out cases mishandled by the SBI crime lab and the "years of warnings."

"Bad Science" Timeline of Key Cases

1991	Greg Taylor arrested for murder based on false blood evidence
1993	Floyd Brown arrested for murder based on falsified confession
	Lacked capacity to stand trial; held in psychiatric hospital
2003	Michael Peterson found guilty of murder
2005	Alarms raised by treating doctors about Floyd Brown's capacity to make confession
2007	Kirk Turner arrested for murder
2009	National study by law professors Garret and Neufeld on role of bad forensics in wrongful convictions published in *Virginia Law Review*
	Kirk Turner found not guilty (self-defense)
	Floyd Brown released from psychiatric hospital by judge for lack of evidence
	National report by the National Academies of Sciences published
	Alan Gell awarded $3.9 million from SBI for wrongful conviction
2010	Greg Taylor exonerated by Innocence Commission and pardoned by governor
	48 Hours episode on Kirk Turner case aired in May
	News & Observer series on SBI published in August
	Swecker and Wolf study commissioned by governor
2011	Deaver fired by SBI in January
	New trial ordered for Peterson in December
2012	Swecker and Wolf report released
2016	North Carolina Supreme Court allows Kirk Turner's civil lawsuit to proceed against SBI agents Duane Deaver and Gerald Thomas
2017	Michael Peterson makes an Alford plea to voluntary manslaughter and is released for time served
2018	Kirk Turner's civil lawsuit settled

Heather Coyle, a DNA expert with the Connecticut state crime lab, had been hired as a defense expert in a North Carolina case. In the *News & Observer* series, she went public with her concerns about the SBI lab: "What they do is hardly science."

As an illustration, DNA is one area where statistical analysis is the norm and standards were adopted early in its forensic use. DNA analysis should be one of the most reliable forensic tests. But while DNA examiners in Connecticut require three or four consistent identifiers when a crime scene has mixed samples, North Carolina's examiners declared a match if only one of the sixteen identifiers matched a suspect. One veteran SBI examiner said, "There are no minimum standards as far as I'm concerned."

The situation could no longer be ignored. After Greg Taylor's exoneration and pardon in 2010, the state's then–attorney general Roy Cooper took action. He brought in former FBI agents Chris Swecker and Michael Wolf to evaluate the SBI lab's biology section. Swecker, a veteran of high-profile investigations, including the Olympic Park bombing in Atlanta and a Hezbollah cigarette-smuggling ring, had served in high-ranking positions in the FBI. Wolf had a forensic lab background and had also served as an FBI agent and director.

The report from their fifteen-month study was released in 2012. They identified 230 cases with profiles similar to Greg Taylor's case. Duane Deaver was linked to thirty-four of those cases. He also served as an SBI training officer, which inevitably helped set the culture for that section of the lab.

The report emphasized that it wasn't an indictment of the SBI lab as a whole; it focused only on lab findings similar to those in the Taylor case. The cases identified as flawed needed further review. Records should be computerized so they could be more easily shared with attorneys on both sides.

The avalanche of investigations into crime labs wasn't limited to North Carolina. Those in forensics leadership positions around the country had long called for more standardized processes, lab inspections, observations of analysts and technicians at work and separating labs from law enforcement. Science, after all, should be objective and impartial, not linked to the prosecutor and the making of cases against defendants.

The repercussions of state and national reports and of growing numbers of DNA exonerations would play out in one particularly high-profile North Carolina case: Duane Deaver's testimony in the murder conviction of Michael Peterson.

MICHAEL PETERSON

Only one other North Carolina case has drawn as much national attention and been as hotly debated as Michael Peterson's—that of Dr. Jeffrey MacDonald, the army surgeon convicted in the 1970 murders of his wife and two daughters at Fort Bragg. MacDonald's case has been the subject of books, movies, TV interviews, documentaries, appeals, convoluted court proceedings and persistent assertions of innocence.

Michael Peterson was also a military officer—a Marine captain. He shared a spotlight similar to MacDonald's, accused of killing his wife, with plenty of news coverage and courtroom drama. The major difference was that Peterson's case started thirty years after MacDonald's, so Peterson's played out in front of new media unavailable in the 1970s.

MacDonald asked journalist Joe McGinniss if he'd be interested in writing a book and granted access during his trial preparation. The 1983 book *Fatal Vision* recounted McGinniss's insider view of the trial.

In Peterson's case, the defense granted access to a French filmmaker, Jean-Xavier de Lestrade, who followed the trial preparations and created what eventually became Netflix's *The Staircase*.

The details are well-known: Peterson, a Vietnam-era warrior, became a best-selling novelist and political gadfly in Durham and was married to a Nortel executive. Their blended family lived in a 9,500-square-foot mansion in a toney part of Durham. Their home hosted warm, inviting dinner parties, pulled together by the sociable, accomplished and brainy Kathleen Peterson—the first woman admitted to Duke's engineering school.

Their story changed dramatically on December 9, 2001, when Peterson called 911 to report he'd found his wife unconscious at the bottom of the back stairs in their home.

The original trial, even without what became the behind-the-scenes documentary of the defense's story, was must-see TV. A male prostitute and a steamy email exchange with Michael Peterson; battling experts arguing the couple's financial well-being or distress; famed criminologist Henry Lee spitting ketchup in the courtroom; the Peterson friend in Germany also found dead at the bottom of a staircase, with similar head wounds; an exhumation in Texas; effective and hard-fighting lawyers on both sides; and Peterson's sons and adopted daughters and Kathleen's daughter and sister looking on and choosing their sides—these all added up to compelling drama in what was, at the time, North Carolina's longest-running trial.

In October 2003, after deliberating for four days, the jury found Peterson guilty of first-degree murder. He was sentenced to life in prison.

In 2007, Peterson agreed to settle the civil wrongful death lawsuit brought by Kathleen's daughter, Caitlin Atwater. The $25 million award seemed largely symbolic, given his prison sentence and lack of assets.

Peterson's appeals proved unsuccessful—until the issues with the SBI lab became public.

Above: Gates at the drive into the former Peterson home in Durham. Note: This is a private residence. *Photo courtesy of Robert Finley.*

Opposite: Entrance to the State Bureau of Investigation's Crime Lab in Raleigh. *Photo by Cathy Pickens.*

Duane Deaver had been a key prosecution witness. In fact, the prosecutor identified Deaver's testimony as "obviously central to this case" in his closing argument.

In 2011, Judge Orlando Hudson held a hearing on a Motion for Appropriate Relief (MAR) filed by Peterson's attorney seeking a new trial. The MAR summarized Deaver's critical role in the case: "The prosecution witnesses claimed that the injuries were consistent with a beating and

inconsistent with an accident; the defense witnesses testified that the injuries were consistent with an accident and inconsistent with a beating. But only one alleged 'expert' testified that it was Michael Peterson who had beaten Kathleen Peterson to death. That 'expert' was former SBI Agent Duane Deaver, who based his testimony on his interpretation of bloodstains found in the area of the stairway and bloodstains on Michael Peterson's shorts and sneakers."

In the hearing, forensic expert Tim Palmbach, another coauthor with Dr. Henry Lee and a former director of the Connecticut Forensic Science Laboratory, testified that Deaver's own supervisor noted his troubling "bias toward the prosecution." Of Deaver's "experiments" to duplicate the blood found on Peterson's clothes, Palmbach said Deaver's work "failed to meet the basic rules governing high-school science," that he failed to document his work and failed to test competing hypotheses, instead designing the experiments to prove the outcome he wanted. In short, the science wasn't science.

The defense experts found the blood spatter more consistent with a fall but, as proof of their objectivity, they couldn't rule out some of the spatter coming from an intentional injury rather than an accident. Science couldn't show with "certainty" whether Kathleen had fallen or was battered, only that the blood evidence was, in the defense opinion, more consistent with a fall.

Following the hearing, Judge Hudson granted the motion, allowing Peterson a new trial.

In a comment to Raleigh journalist Jeff Neff, UNC law school professor Joseph Kennedy found Deaver's conduct "mind-boggling." The case had no eyewitness, no confession, only the circumstances and the forensics. "To perjure oneself as an expert in a circumstantial murder trial is the gravest sort of perjury," Kennedy said.

The prosecutor could retry the case, but that decision dragged on for several years until, in 2017, Peterson agreed to accept an Alford plea. In exchange for admitting the state had enough evidence to convict him of

Durham County Courthouse. *Photo courtesy of the North Carolina Judicial Branch.*

voluntary manslaughter—a significantly reduced charge from first-degree murder—but without having to admit guilt, Peterson walked free. Judge Hudson sentenced him to a maximum of just over seven years, with credit for seven years he'd already served.

Of course, he remained a convicted felon and he still faced the $25 million civil verdict, should he ever make any money. But he was no longer in Nash Correctional Institution.

In 2019, Peterson published his memoir, with vivid stories of the trial, his time in prison and the aftermath. He self-published it and donated the proceeds to charity to steer clear of the civil judgment.

The Staircase aired on Netflix to a wide audience. The *Behind the Staircase* website (https://www.peterson-staircase.com/index.html) pointed out problems with the documentary's viewpoint. Within the two families and among interested court watchers, the lines are firmly drawn.

The case illustrated the real danger when an expert puts a thumb on the scale of justice to help the state prove its case. Society rightly fears a rigged system.

4

THE POISONERS

A Modern-Day Arsenic Mystery

Some cases draw interest because they are studies in contrast. Picture the modern-day Research Triangle full of scientists, researchers and medical specialists, sleek modern buildings, gleaming equipment, first-rate minds bent on using technology to solve problems and save the world. Contrast that with a tale from a fusty Golden Age murder mystery, but instead of arsenic and old lace, you find arsenic and bowling and beer.

A twenty-first-century arsenic poisoning? Wouldn't that be an anachronism one hundred years past its prime—with a cast of characters better suited to a science thriller than an Agatha Christie novel?

In February 2001, *Charlotte Observer* reporter Tim Whitmire noted poisoning caused a minuscule number of homicide deaths, "just 11 of 12,658 in 1999, according to the FBI's Uniform Crime Report." But is that just the tip of an iceberg of unseen cases? Poison expert John Trestrail suggested it was: "If all the people we have in our cemeteries who had been poisoned could raise their hands, we would probably be shocked by the numbers."

Perhaps in this Raleigh case, the killer figured old methods work best.

Whether in a Christie novel or a modern-day poison puzzle, such a crime often begins with someone facing a problem that seems intractable. That problem is too often an inconvenient spouse. Even when reasons are offered for such an act, they rarely explain what happened, much as those affected might wish they could. Putting its curiosities aside, at its sober heart, this story involved two little girls who lost their daddies and families who lost smart, successful, much-loved sons and brothers.

As old-fashioned as arsenic might seem as a murder weapon, it has remained a popular choice for centuries for a reason: it is cheap, easily obtained (even in an age of digital recordkeeping), effective and—very important to one who doesn't want to get caught—often still confused with other, innocent causes of death.

In this Raleigh case, the arsenic masqueraded, as it often does, as severe gastroenteritis, severe enough to send Dr. Eric Miller to Raleigh's Rex Hospital early on the morning of November 16, 2000, where he was admitted to intensive care when his condition didn't improve. Still later, he was transferred to the University of North Carolina hospital in Chapel Hill.

Eric Miller had met and fallen in love with Ann Brier while attending Perdue University. He'd grown up in Indiana, and she came from a small town in Pennsylvania. They were both smart and athletic, both majoring in chemistry. When they graduated, they married and moved together to Raleigh for graduate work at North Carolina State University. Eric received his PhD in 1998. Though tempted by a well-paying industry job, he instead accepted a less-lucrative position doing pediatric AIDS research under a federal grant.

Ann left her doctoral studies and, with her master's degree in biochemistry, began working with a large pharmaceutical company. She gave birth to their daughter in early 2000.

On the evening of November 15, the night before his hospital admission, Eric got together with Derril Willard and some of Ann's other coworkers at a bowling alley. Ann's work group often met for bowling evenings; she had attended and brought Eric with her in the past. On this evening, Eric attended without her.

At one point, Willard went to the snack bar, bought a pitcher of beer and served everyone a glass.

Eric commented that the beer tasted "funky." Another of the guys tasted his and said, "It's just bowling alley beer." Later in the evening, Eric became violently ill, throwing up in a bag while trying to continue bowling.

The episodes didn't abate through the night. Early the next morning, Ann took him to Rex Hospital in Raleigh.

Eric and the doctors assumed he had contracted a stomach bug or food poisoning, though the doctors were surprised at such violent symptoms from food poisoning. They ran through their testing protocols, trying to identify what was making him so sick.

Emergency entrance of Rex Hospital where Eric Miller was first treated. *Photo by Cathy Pickens.*

He stayed in the hospital for over a week, with doctors still not confident about the cause. Trying to work through the possible causes, a doctor had ordered a heavy metals test, just before Eric was transferred from Rex Hospital's ICU to the University of North Carolina hospital. The UNC hospital had more sophisticated equipment on hand.

Readers of classic mystery fiction would say, "How obvious! It must be poison!" But physicians see far more cases of bacterial or viral gastroenteritis coming through their doors than they see poisoning, whether deliberate or accidental.

Those who expect poisoning because they've read plenty of mystery novels don't expect toxicology reports to take days or weeks. But they do.

In this case, the wait was compounded by an error on the report that made the findings look less important than they were, so the doctors at UNC weren't immediately aware of the serious implications of the heavy metals test.

On November 24, after ten days, Eric recovered enough to go home, with the cause still unknown—not an unusual outcome with food poisoning or other gastric ailments. His parents came to Raleigh to help nurse him and care for their baby granddaughter while Ann worked.

Eric's health and strength continued to improve enough for him to take a short walk, so on the night of November 30, his parents decided to take a break and enjoy an evening out. Ann heated up some chicken and rice for Eric's supper.

That night, Eric's gastrointestinal symptoms returned with a vengeance, and he was forced to return to the hospital the next day.

The error in recording the heavy metals test ordered during his first hospital stay was discovered. Eric's toxicology screen showed he had ingested a massive amount of arsenic before his first hospitalization.

Eric Miller's neighborhood where he felt well enough to walk the day before his last trip to the hospital. *Photo by Cathy Pickens.*

Doctors now knew the cause of his illness. But how had the arsenic gotten into his system?

Enter the Raleigh Police Department.

Investigators arrived at the hospital, but Eric had no clue what had happened or how he'd ingested arsenic. Early on the morning of December 2, with his wife, Ann, at his side, Eric Miller died, roughly two weeks after she first took him to the hospital.

Raleigh police had not learned anything helpful from Eric before he died. But they knew they were dealing with arsenic poisoning. As with most poisoning cases, the cause is only part of the puzzle. What was the source of the poison? Did someone administer it? Those are questions seldom easily answered.

Police first searched the Miller home for arsenic. Then, with a search warrant, they searched Ann Miller's workplace, where they took her computer, expense reports and other documents. They also found sodium cacodylate, an arsenic compound often used in lab research. They obtained Eric's emails and lab computer files.

Ann wasn't answering any police questions, and within days, she had hired a lawyer—Wade Smith, a gentlemanly and deadly effective criminal defense lawyer.

Even though she wasn't speaking to investigators, her email files told them plenty. It quickly became clear she had extramarital relationships with at least two men. One was Derril Willard, her coworker.

Their workplace relationship had changed to something more intimate sometime in the fall of 2000. In November, the two traveled to Chicago one weekend, ostensibly on a work trip. They checked into the Ritz-Carlton as husband and wife. The following week, Eric became ill at the bowling alley.

Ann also reportedly had a three-year affair with a research scientist at the University of California–San Francisco. Their last rendezvous was in May 1999, a trip to North Carolina's Outer Banks. Ann paid for the hotel and his airfare from California. He later told Chris Morgan, a Raleigh detective, that he wouldn't have taken the trip if he'd had to pay for it. He wasn't as invested in the relationship as Ann was.

Investigators were learning Ann Miller wasn't the demure, churchgoing perfectionist she presented. But was she a murderer? And could they prove it?

At this point, the case appeared to be an ordinary love triangle gone bad. Then it took unexpected turns, leading to a landmark judicial decision and yet more tragedy.

Unbeknownst to investigators, six days after Eric's death, Derril Willard met with Durham defense attorney Rick Gammon. As happens in cities like Raleigh and Durham that still retain much of their small-town character, Gammon, a former police officer, was also a longtime friend of homicide investigator Chris Morgan.

At least two of Morgan's homicide investigations have been recounted on national TV news documentaries. With his ever-present fedora and his slow, husky voice, he's a good storyteller—and he's the image of a bulldog investigator.

When the Miller investigation began, Morgan was not the lead detective. He did, however, doggedly nose around the edges, feeling more could be done. His persistence was a tactic that did not always endear Morgan to his colleagues but was one that often got results.

On January 21, Morgan was the investigator assigned to knock on Derril Willard's door with a search warrant.

Another Tragedy

The revelations in Ann's work emails led to a warrant to search Willard's home, the kind of methodical trail-following required in a complicated case.

Others know how to follow trails, too. Morgan knew the diligent Raleigh *News & Observer* reporter Oren Dorell was a "well-known 'search-warrant grazer.'" Dorell would comb through search warrants, which were public information. The application for a search warrant contains details needed to show probable cause for a search. In the warrant applications, Dorell often found key pieces to a story police weren't sharing in interviews. In this case, the warrant application would alert the press to Willard's involvement and to the funky beer at the bowling alley.

So, police timed the search to occur as soon as the warrant was signed, before the story had time to hit the newspaper.

Willard answered the door. The two men had a quick conversation while sitting outside in Morgan's car. Morgan was blunt: "I think you've been used by a woman."

Willard said, "Yeah, and she's done a good job of it." Willard said nothing more, but Morgan knew he was on the right track.

As expected, news of the search and what the police were looking for appeared above the fold in the Raleigh newspaper the next morning.

The day the news broke, Willard's wife drove up to their house, opened the garage, and found Derril dead of a self-inflicted gunshot wound. Like Eric Miller, he left behind a wife and young daughter.

Tacked on the wall of the garage, he left a suicide note, which read in part, "I have taken no one else's life but my own."

Sitting in Morgan's car the day before, Willard had borrowed Detective Morgan's phone to call his attorney, Rick Gammon, a former police officer and friend of Morgan's.

After Willard's death, Morgan immediately assumed what any experienced detective would—that Derril Willard had hired an attorney *before* any contact with the police because he had something to hide. He also figured Willard told his lawyer something important about Eric Miller's poisoning. Why else go to a lawyer and later commit suicide?

From early in the investigation, Morgan suspected Ann Miller in her husband's death. He followed the rule to always look first at those closest to the victim. The rule certainly applies in poisoning cases where intimate contact with food and drink is critical. But the investigation had thus far failed to build a strong enough case to arrest Ann.

Two months after Eric's death, the story was spreading beyond Raleigh and Durham. The Charlotte newspaper ran a front-page summary of key facts: the searches of the Miller and Willard houses and that Miller had first been hospitalized after drinking with Willard and then again after eating a meal at home with Ann. But investigators were still keeping much of what they knew quiet.

The full results of the autopsy and toxicology evaluation took five months to complete. In advance of the May 10 and May 16 reports, police knew the information would explode coverage of the case. Reporters closely followed this case. And why wouldn't they? A handsome, personable young father, a researcher dedicated to battling childhood AIDS, dies of arsenic poisoning? People wanted to know what happened.

Investigators, the judge and the district attorney didn't want any missteps in building a viable case. After the publicity around the search warrants, a judge agreed to seal the autopsy report for a period of time.

The reason for sealing the autopsy report later became clear—it showed Eric Miller had been ingesting doses of arsenic for five or six months before his death.

The results were shocking. Eric's poisoning hadn't been a one-time event. He'd apparently received small doses starting in June 2000. The doses were enough to make him slightly ill, which coincided with Eric's periodic complaints of stomach problems over those months.

Therefore, whoever administered the poison had to be someone with access to Eric and his food over a period of time. The most likely suspect, of course, was his wife.

Ann, the one person detectives most wanted to talk to, left Raleigh. After Willard's death, she and her young daughter moved to Wilmington, North Carolina, to live near Ann's sister. The need for family support was understandable. At first, she worked at a home design store, a job far removed from her pharmaceutical research.

With their suspect no longer close at hand, Morgan and other investigators continued to follow every lead and ask every possible question. But too little was happening in the case.

During this period, Morgan was promoted to a position where he no longer had to stay on the sidelines of the investigation. He felt Ann should be under surveillance. That was harder to do, with her two hours away in Wilmington, but for periods, he decided he and other officers would take turns in Wilmington, staking out her house and keeping tabs on her movements.

They learned she was working again with a small pharmaceutical company. And she was apparently spending time with a new man who worked as an electrician and a musician in a Christian rock band.

Experienced prosecutors are leery of bringing charges too early, especially in complicated cases where proof relies on circumstantial rather than direct evidence. No one could put the poison in Ann's hands. No one saw the poison administered. No one could testify about who administered the poison and when. Proving motive is not a requirement in a murder case, but jurors would still want some plausible explanation for why a wife would want to destroy her apparently loving husband.

If prosecutors charge the wrong person and later learn someone else committed the crime, prosecuting the real perpetrator will be difficult. Any defense attorney would delight in asking, "You got it wrong once, how do we know you haven't made a mistake this time?"

In addition, if charges are brought and the available evidence doesn't convince the jury, a killer can walk free and, thanks to constitutional protections against double jeopardy, can't be tried again. Even if a photo of the actual murder taking place surfaced later, an acquitted killer can't be retried.

So, prosecutors learn to demand ever more proof and to relentlessly cross-examine investigators, looking for the holes and weaknesses a defense attorney could ferret out.

Poisoning cases are difficult to prove. Sure, tests show the poison is present in the deceased's system. But poison may not be ingested immediately, so the killer need not be present on the scene of the murder. Poison is sneaky, stealthy and can be done at a distance or over a period of time. The prosecutor in this case was careful, wanting to make sure the evidence was solid, persuasive, unassailable.

Chris Morgan believed Derril Willard was a linchpin. But Derril Willard killed himself just weeks after the murder, the day after police brought a warrant to search his house. Morgan wanted the next best thing—he wanted to know what Willard told his attorney.

So, he asked Rick Gammon.

Drawing on their friendship, Detective Morgan personally asked Gammon to tell him what Willard said about the murder. After all, his client was dead. But Gammon refused to breach his client's confidentiality. He wouldn't talk about Derril Willard without a court order.

Morgan was nothing if not persistent. He was convinced Willard had passed on key evidence. Finally, in February 2002, more than a year after Eric's death, the prosecutor asked a judge to compel Gammon to reveal what Derril Willard told him about anyone who had harmed Eric Miller or intended to harm him.

Privileged Communications

Certain professional relationships have long been granted special protections: doctor-patient, priest-penitent and attorney-client. In those situations, those seeking advice may reveal information that could harm their reputations or well-being or endanger their freedom if revealed to the public. But seekers need good counsel for medical, spiritual or legal matters, and they can get good counsel only if they are guaranteed the privilege to reveal themselves and their problems freely and openly to a trusted adviser.

Arguments periodically surface about whether those relationships deserve to be protected—or maybe, in just a special case, whether the rules should be broken. But in general, society believes in shielding these three key relationships from prying eyes.

For North Carolina attorneys, their Rules of Professional Conduct require they protect their clients' confidential information. Under Rule 1.6, an attorney can reveal a client's information only if the client consents or to prevent a client's future crimes or to prevent "reasonably certain death or bodily harm."

The duty to protect client confidentiality continues beyond the grave. In Arizona in the 1970s, William Macumber was charged with two counts of first-degree murder. However, two lawyers in another case had a client who told them he was the one who killed the victims—Macumber had nothing to do with it.

After their client died, the two attorneys were willing to testify about his confession. A state bar association ethics advisory opinion held that they could be allowed to testify. The trial judge, though, disagreed and would not allow the lawyers' testimony.

The wrongly accused Macumber was convicted and sentenced to life in prison. The Arizona Supreme Court upheld the judge's decision, saying the attorneys could not testify about their client's confidential statements, even after his death. After thirty-seven years, Macumber was released thanks to work by the Justice Project but ended up reoffending and rearrested in less than a year.

Why allow an innocent man to sit in prison when reputable witnesses heard the truth from a killer's mouth? The rules protect confidentiality even in such difficult circumstances.

However, in difficult cases, public sentiment might not agree with this reasoning. In one survey, respondents were given a hypothetical: If an attorney has information from a client that would exonerate someone falsely accused, should the attorney reveal the information? Among the public, 80 percent said yes, it should be revealed. Only 19 percent said they would not be willing to consult a lawyer who revealed such information. Of the lawyers questioned, 65 percent said they would disclose the information even though the rules forbid it.

In an independent poll for the *Raleigh News & Observer*, among voters statewide, 48 percent felt lawyers should be forced to reveal what their clients told them in order to help solve a crime, while 32 percent (more women than men, more Black people than white) said no, they shouldn't be forced to. And 20 percent didn't know what should be done. (The North Carolina poll was conducted during the Miller proceedings but did not specifically ask about the case.)

So why doesn't the lawyer just do what's morally right, even if it's not legal?

A lawyer who violates a client's confidentiality can be sued for money damages and lose the license to practice law.

Lake Pleasant Bodies *Case*

Attorneys who staunchly defend their clients' rights are seldom seen as heroes. After all, their clients are at least suspected of doing something wrong.

To explore the nature of professional responsibility, Harvard Business School developed a discussion case for business students—*The Lake Pleasant Bodies*. The Harvard case was based on attorney Frank Armani's decision to take a case he wished he'd passed on.

Armani had represented Robert Garrow once, in an automobile accident case. After that, whenever he got in serious trouble, Garrow wanted no other lawyer, even though Armani didn't handle criminal cases.

In July 1973, Robert Garrow attacked four young people on a camping trip in upstate New York. He forced one victim to tie another to a tree and then he took the three others farther into the woods and repeated the ritual. One broke away and went for help. Carol Ann Malinowski, tied up and left alone, heard her friend Phil Domblewski's screams. She struggled and freed herself and ran to hide in the woods. Later, when help arrived, they found Carol Ann sitting beside Phil's lifeless body. He'd been tortured and stabbed repeatedly.

The young people quickly identified Robert Garrow in a photo lineup. The police moved with a sense of urgency because Garrow was also a suspect in the death of Daniel Porter, a Boston College student, and the kidnapping of his companion, Susan Petz. Porter had been tied up and stabbed; Petz was still missing after nine days, with hope for her safe return fading.

When Garrow was finally captured, one of his first phone calls was to Frank Armani. Following his first consultation about the car wreck case, Garrow had called Armani on other cases—a marijuana possession and false imprisonment charge that was dismissed and, later, an accusation of child sexual molestation involving two ten- and eleven-year-old girls. Armani was beginning to have doubts about Garrow, who had once been touted as a "poster boy" for rehabilitation efforts in the New York State parole system. But Armani also had questions about what looked like some overzealous police work in the molestation case, so he agreed to represent Garrow in this case.

Following the Domblewski and Porter murders, the more Armani found out about Garrow, the more disturbed he was about his client.

Garrow eventually admitted to Armani and another lawyer that he'd held Susan Petz hostage for several days in a tent near his parents' house. When he described her attempt to escape, he seemed genuinely surprised, telling his lawyers that they'd had "great conversations." He stabbed her repeatedly and threw her body down an old mine shaft.

Garrow also surprised them by admitting to another kidnapping, rape and murder—sixteen-year-old Alicia Hauck had been missing for several months. He had raped and killed her, hiding her body in the woods at the edge of a cemetery near Syracuse University.

To check their client's veracity and to gather evidence that might help them build an insanity defense, the attorneys went in search of the mine shaft and cemetery sites. After some searching, they found both bodies, taking pictures but not reporting the bodies' existence or the locations to the police.

In its retelling of the events, the Harvard Business School case presents students with a dilemma to debate, ending with Armani sitting across from Susan Petz's father as Mr. Petz begs Armani for information on his daughter. The Petz family did not know whether their daughter was alive or what had happened to her.

Armani later talked openly about the torment he felt as he faced Petz. On a PBS interview years later, he said, "Your mind's screaming one way, 'Relieve these parents'…and the other is your sworn duty." Armani did not reveal the location of Petz's and Hauck's bodies, maintaining that his client's confidentiality had to be his first concern.

The Armani family's collegial hometown began to feel like a scene from a *Frankenstein* movie, just short of angry villagers storming the castle with torches and pitchforks. Those outraged about Garrow brought their anger to the only person they could find to hold responsible. Armani got death threats and a rock thrown through his window. His wife finally left and took the children to another town to protect them. His business dwindled; he lost partners and clients and replaced his secretary with an answering machine.

At one point, Garrow even sued Armani for $5 million for denying him due process.

Ultimately, Garrow was convicted and was later shot to death during an escape attempt from prison.

Announcing Garrow's death on the nightly news, Roger Mudd summarized: "The public and the legal profession are still strongly divided on the issue of how far an attorney may go in protecting his client's right of confidentiality. On the one hand, an attorney is an officer of the law, he's the committed advocate for a client whose interests often may clash with the law. Which obligation comes first? It is an emotionally charged issue."

It took years for Armani's law practice to recover. "I tried to talk my daughter out of becoming a lawyer," he said. "It's just not what it used to be, as a profession." But he still sounded proud of her—maybe rightly worried about what she might one day face, but proud.

Paragraph 12

In the Miller case, attorney Gammon upheld his professional oath. His client was dead, but Willard left a family. Others could be hurt. And why should future clients trust him if he violated the confidences of Derril Willard?

The district attorney's petition to force Gammon to reveal what Willard told him bounced back and forth in the courts. The appellate court eventually held that Gammon must provide a very limited statement of what his client said. From the sheaf of notes Gammon presented to the court, the court ordered the release of only one paragraph, what became known as Paragraph 12.

Gammon hand-delivered Paragraph 12 in a sealed envelope:

> *Mr. Willard then stated that on one recent occasion he had met Mrs. Miller in a parking lot, and they had a conversation while in an SUV. He stated that during his conversation Mrs. Miller was crying and that she told him she had been to the hospital where Mr. Miller had been admitted. She stated to Mr. Willard that she was by herself in the room with Mr. Miller for a period of time. She then told Mr. Willard that she took a syringe and needle*

from her purse and injected the contents of the syringe into Mr. Miller's IV. Upon being questioned as to the contents of the syringe, Mr. Willard either stated that the substance was from work, or that Mrs. Miller told him it was from work. He then stated that he asked Mrs. Miller why she had done this, and she replied, "I don't know." Mr. Willard surmised that Mrs. Miller was attempting to end Mr. Miller's suffering from his illness with these actions. Although Mr. Gammon and Mr. Fitzhugh do not recall specifically whether Mr. Willard or Mrs. Miller used the word "arsenic" with reference to the contents of the syringe, it was clear that the substance contained in the syringe was poisonous. Mr. Willard then stated he knew nothing further of the circumstances surrounding Eric Miller's death. He also stated that he had not told anyone including his wife, about Mrs. Miller's statements to him.

In the end, Willard's statements damaged not himself but Ann Miller. She had confessed to him that she injected a poisonous "substance" into Eric's IV line while he lay in the hospital.

The statement gave the prosecutor sufficient grounds to file charges. Ann turned herself in.

At her bond hearing, Chris Morgan said Ann showed up in court that day looking as if she "had every expectation of going home." Ann, as well as Eric's family, heard for the first time what had been revealed in Gammon's Paragraph 12.

Wade Smith and Joseph Cheshire, Ann's skillful, respected and expensive defense attorneys, were well-known. Both had represented young men involved in the Duke lacrosse case. Both were known as the attorneys one called when one was in trouble.

Her attorneys made good arguments about why she should be released—that she was a mother, she hadn't fled, she had family support and no criminal history. The judge ordered her held on a $3 million bond. Technically, she was awarded a bond, just one she couldn't meet.

Ann returned to jail awaiting her trial date and made no comments and gave no details to investigators.

Plea Deal

Ann never went to trial. Instead, in November 2005, five years after Eric's death, she accepted a deal, pleaded guilty to murder and conspiracy and was sentenced to between twenty-five and thirty-one years in prison.

Wake County district attorney Colon Willoughby offered the plea deal because circumstantial evidence cases can be difficult to present to jurors. Willard was not available to testify, and his statement was a key to understanding what had happened. Those involved in the prosecution worried that Ann, who had been described as chameleon-like and convincing, might persuade a jury that a well-educated young mother couldn't have murdered her husband.

Defense attorney Joseph Cheshire read a statement about her "deep sense of remorse and regret." She will be at least sixty years old before she is eligible for release.

The lack of a confession or any public insight left court watchers with only speculation about the motive. Detective Morgan didn't see a mother as attached to her child as he expected. In the end, Morgan felt she lacked empathy, that her life was a matter of putting on the right appearance. Her real motivation was always her own needs; she really couldn't see or empathize with others. Morgan admits that is just his speculation. Sometimes the tough questions don't get answered.

Whatever the motive, two little girls were left without daddies who adored them. Family members were left without men they loved and still miss.

In the aftermath, Derril Willard's widow said, "She's admitting responsibility for what she did to Eric, but she's not admitting what she did to Derril. That really makes me angry and sad."

Statistically, most poisoners—though not all—are women. With her plea, Ann Miller joined a noteworthy list of North Carolina's convicted female arsenic poisoners: Nannie Doss, Velma Barfield and Blanche Taylor Moore.

INSULIN POISON

While deadly and easy to obtain, insulin rarely appears as a murder weapon—whether the murder is attempted, suspected or proved, according to Dr. Vincent Marks, a world-renowned expert. In 2009, his research found only sixty-six insulin murder cases worldwide. Fewer than half led to a conviction, and an additional weapon was used in eleven of the cases.

The most sensational insulin case was that of Claus von Bülow for the attempted murder of his wife, Sunny. A criminal trial peeking behind the drapes of the rich and famous? The first televised case with insulin as the weapon? Naturally, it attracted attention. Sunny von Bülow remained in a coma, and sordid family secrets filled the headlines as her husband stood trial in 1982. He was convicted of injecting her with insulin and sentenced to thirty years in prison.

In a second trial in 1985, based in part on more detailed scientific evidence about the effects of alcohol use and hypoglycemia presented by a who's who of medical specialists, including Dr. Marks, von Bülow was acquitted.

As the von Bülow case illustrated, proving murder by insulin is complicated.

In Sanford, without the von Bülow aura of high society and mega-wealth, North Carolina prosecutors faced similar difficulties proving murder by insulin. Did the September 1986 death of Roy Wayne Gilmore result from a deadly insulin injection? If so, who administered it? Three separate juries wrestled with answering those questions.

Prosecutors believed Gilmore's wife, Eunice, and his son, Roy Wayne Gilmore Jr., conspired to kill the forty-seven-year-old with insulin. Gilmore Sr. was injected at least twice while at his home, the first injection in the early morning hours of August 29, 1986, the second around five that evening, ten to fourteen hours after the first injection. He died a week later at Duke University Hospital.

Murder by insulin is rare because, frankly, the body defends itself well from the dangerous drop in blood sugar caused by too much insulin. Insulin, which regulates blood sugar, naturally occurs in healthy people. Patients who receive too much insulin can recover quickly simply by eating and drinking.

According to Dr. Vincent Marks, a chemical pathologist and researcher from the United Kingdom, the symptoms of insulin poisoning are the same as those of hypoglycemia or low blood sugar: sweating, anxiety, blurred vision, rapid heartbeat and general malaise. Any diabetic has experienced these symptoms at some time. If not addressed, coma can result.

Or, in the case of Ray Gilmore, if more insulin is injected than a non-diabetic can process, a coma can result, followed by multiple organ failure.

The very young and the very old are more susceptible to deadly drops in blood sugar. Professor Marks points out, "It takes about six hours after the patient becomes comatose from lack of glucose in their blood before it produces permanent brain damage," if the patient is left untreated. Because the body's reaction to insulin allows time for a victim to be discovered and get help, Professor Marks doesn't consider it a perfect murder weapon. Most victims survive with treatment.

However, insulin can be a perfect murder weapon for other reasons. Because insulin occurs naturally in the body, postmortem exams can't pinpoint the exact amount injected—a therapeutic amount or a lethal amount. Because the body's response to insulin develops over several hours and varies from person to person, pinpointing who had the opportunity to give the injection is also tricky. Close relatives and caregivers are naturally the most likely suspects, but time frames and access are critical.

The published reports in the Gilmore case indicate no courtroom debate over what killed him. Insulin was the culprit. The appellate case and scant news coverage mentioned no concern about accidental overdose. Instead, the arguments centered on who administered it and who was nearby and acting "in concert" in the murder.

Eunice Gilmore was a nurse and shared a home with her husband. Their son's home was just behind theirs. On the day of the poisoning, Roy Jr. was in and out of his parents' house. Were both involved? Or only one?

Poisonings require painstaking investigation. Charges against mother and son in Gilmore's death weren't brought until March 1987, more than six months after his death.

Roy Jr. was the first defendant brought to trial, in September 1988.

Roy Sr.'s mother and some of his brothers and sisters testified at the trial. They said Eunice had tried to remove Gilmore from Duke University Hospital, where he was being treated, and take him back to Sanford. They also testified that she'd tried to keep his family away from him and she'd been "adamant that there be no autopsy."

Lee County Courthouse in Sanford, where Gilmore trial was held. *Photo courtesy of the North Carolina Judicial Branch.*

To counter Mr. Gilmore's family, Roy Jr.'s defense pointed out how these family members would benefit if mother and son were convicted of murder, since under North Carolina's "slayer statute," they couldn't inherit anything if they'd killed him. If they were convicted, Mr. Gilmore's estate would instead go to his mother and, depending on her estate plans, to his brothers and sisters. The defense attorney argued that the possible inheritance gave Roy Jr.'s grandmother and uncles and aunts some motive for making sure he and his mother got convicted.

That point failed to carry the day, either in the trial court or on appeal.

Roy Jr.'s girlfriend testified that when she woke at about eleven o'clock in the morning, Roy Jr. wasn't in the house. Minutes later, he came in, saying he'd been to his dad's house to use the phone. The girlfriend said he returned to his dad's house for about thirty minutes around one o'clock.

Roy Jr. had been incarcerated earlier in 1986, serving time on another charge. A fellow inmate testified that Roy Jr. talked about his dad "running around" on his mom and "it was going to get him killed."

Another inmate testified that Roy Jr. admitted he'd "masterminded" his father's death. He and his mother had decided on insulin rather than a pistol because it was less messy. He also said he'd be getting $100,000 in insurance money. He said his mother had given the first injection. He'd checked on his dad in the afternoon to see if he was "dead or almost dead," and he'd been the one who got rid of the syringes.

Roy Jr. faced a first-degree murder charge because he acted in concert with his mother in the plot. When deciding whether he'd done it for the money—which would have raised the stakes to a possible death penalty—the jury said no. As a result, in September 1988, Roy Gilmore Jr. was convicted in the insulin poisoning death of his father and sentenced to life in prison.

On appeal, the North Carolina Supreme Court recognized the difficulty of pinpointing precisely when the two injections occurred and who held the syringe. They decided Roy Jr. did not have to be on the scene or carry out "all of the acts necessary to constitute the crime." The back of Roy Jr.'s house faced the back of his parents' house. Stepping out his back door put him in his parents' backyard. The court found even when Roy Jr. was in his own home, he was "in close enough proximity to the scene of the murder to be able to render assistance to his mother in committing the crime if needed."

Of course, he also could have helped his father, had he wished to do so. But that was not what happened.

The following April, his mother's trial began. She testified her husband woke up during the night of August 29. He complained of being dizzy and

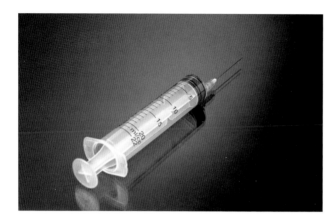

Syringe. *Image courtesy of Dmitriy, ds_30 on Pixabay.*

disoriented, so she gave him candy and orange juice—the standard treatment for a diabetic. The next morning, he stayed home in bed, not feeling well enough to report to his truck-driving job.

Mrs. Gilmore went on to her nursing job. When she came home that afternoon, she found him comatose.

Evidence presented showed Mr. Gilmore was not diabetic and did not take insulin.

Her trial ended in a hung jury, eleven to one for conviction. Her second trial in October 1989 ended only slightly better in her favor: ten to two for conviction. At the conclusion of that trial, James Coman, the senior deputy attorney for the state's criminal division, said if most jurors had reasonable doubt about her guilt, the state would have no reason to retry the case. But since the clear majority of jurors in both trials felt she was guilty, "it would be a miscarriage of justice not to proceed" with a third trial.

However, in 1992, a judge declared the delay in trying her a third time violated her right to a speedy trial, so she could not be tried again. In effect, she was a free woman.

Until her death in 2018, at age seventy-six, Eunice continued to attend the Holly Springs Baptist Church about ten miles outside Sanford, and she kept herself entertained with her poodles and her cross-stitching.

Roy Wayne Gilmore was paroled in 2007.

FREE AND FAMOUS

JOAN LITTLE

Few North Carolina murder cases have attracted as many national headlines or commentators as Joan Little's 1975 trial. In analyzing the case thirty years after it happened, Professor James R. Acker wrote the "case had an undeniable 'mythic quality' and was hailed by some as the preeminent civil rights trial of the 1970s," but "it receded to obscurity almost as rapidly as it had captivated the nation in the summer of 1975." That might be true for the rest of the country, but for plenty of people in North Carolina, Joan Little's case stayed very much close to mind.

Joan (she preferred the pronunciation Jo-Anne) Little grew up in Washington, North Carolina. But Little's case would wind up in Raleigh.

The oldest of nine children, as a teenager, she quickly became "more than her mother could handle," to the point that her mother got the court to commit her to a training school. She ran away.

Her scrapes with the law (including a conviction for breaking and entering, stealing televisions, clothes, a rifle and other goods with her brother, which landed her in jail in 1974), her tendency to escape whenever she could and a willingness to do what it took to provide for herself (working at a disco near Camp Lejeune Marine base) all created a reputation that didn't serve her well with authority figures in Washington.

Twenty-year-old Joan wanted more than her little-town life and high-school-drop-out status afforded her. "She always wanted to be a city girl," her mother said later.

Wake County Courthouse in Raleigh, where Joan Little's case was heard. *Photo courtesy of the North Carolina Judicial Branch.*

Despite her young age and the variety of her run-ins with the law, she seemed an unlikely candidate for setting so many remarkable precedents in so many areas: scientific jury selection, the right of a woman to use deadly force to defend herself from sexual assault, the vulnerability of incarcerated women (Black women in particular), the death penalty debate and the persistence of antebellum mores and prejudices, particularly in rural areas of the Deep South.

Little's case also brought together a dramatic assortment of contrasts: poor versus not quite rich but quite comfortable, Black versus white, North versus South, rural and small-town regions versus urban but modestly sized cities, those who'd been imprisoned versus those who hadn't, those with political agendas beyond Joan Little's interests versus the status quo.

Add to those dramatic contrasts an assortment of characters thrust into their roles: a young, scared, unpredictable Black woman with a history of brushes with the law; a district attorney unaccustomed to the media crush of a politically charged case; activists for women's rights, civil rights and prison reform, all with their new poster child; a flamboyant rebel of a defense attorney who grew up in the same little town as Joan Little and Cecil B. DeMille.

Set the stage in a part of the country struggling to understand if and how it should change, and the Joan Little case was made for the headlines.

The trouble was that regional newspapers in the South couldn't quite bring themselves to tell the worst of the story. And journalists from the North, a world away in time and place, couldn't quite grasp the subtleties of the people, the place or the situation and relied sometimes on stereotype and caricature.

Much of what happened on the evening of August 27, 1974, in the jail inside the Beaufort County Courthouse was fairly settled, not really disputed. The routines were lax in the sheriff's office and jail, housed in the basement of the recently built courthouse. Inmates were allowed to move around outside their cells. That evening, Joan Little asked to use the phone in the office. A teenage male inmate was drinking a soft drink. The jailer on night duty left one or both of them alone in the office while he helped someone wanting to swear out an assault warrant.

How Little's cell looked early the next morning was not really disputed—though newspapers close to home chose not to report every embarrassing detail at the time. They left that to papers such as *The New York Times* and to the autopsy report.

Night jailer Clarence Alligood's shoes were outside the cell. He was locked in the cell, slumped on a blanket folded on the floor. Naked from the waist down except for his socks, he clutched his pants in one hand. An icepick lay

Beaufort County Courthouse in Washington, where Joan Little was held in the basement jail. *Photo courtesy of the North Carolina Judicial Branch.*

in his open hand. He'd been stabbed eleven times, including in his temple, with a fatal wound to his heart.

Joan Little and the jailer's keys were gone.

The local papers didn't report every detail provided in the autopsy report, like the fact that the fluid running down his leg was semen.

Needless to say, *CSI* hadn't yet taught TV audiences the importance of maintaining a crime scene. A deputy took the icepick from Alligood's hand and passed it to another officer, who slipped it in his back pocket. Before SBI agents arrived from Raleigh, the officers had tidied everything up for them, even washing down the cell walls. During the trial, the *News & Observer* reported that an expert witness from New York had jurors "openly laughing" as he described the lapses in procedure: "that fingerprints might have been lifted from an ice pick that had been stuffed in a deputy's pocket; that photos were 'inferior'; and that evidence may have been contaminated by being thrown together in a pillow case."

After her escape, Little hid out in a house just blocks from the county courthouse. She was afraid to show herself, afraid of what would happen. Killing was one thing. Killing a jailer was another. Killing a white jailer was, for Joan Little, dangerous.

Much of what happened during the search for Little stoked fears about her safety. Men went door to door with rifles and dogs, hunting for her. A judge threatened to declare her an "outlaw," which under an oddity of North Carolina law meant anyone could shoot her on sight. The outlaw declaration was never made, and the law was soon declared unconstitutional, but even the threat only confirmed the images of vigilante redneck southerners.

For almost a week, she hid out. Speculation ran rampant. Had she gone to the office to use the phone so she could slip the ice pick from the desk drawer, planning the attack? Or did he bring it to threaten her?

A local woman got in touch with civil rights attorney Jerry Paul, a hometown boy who practiced law in Chapel Hill. Paul spirited Little away from Washington and arranged for her surrender to state police in Raleigh.

Rather than return her to Washington to be held in the jail there, she was sent to Women's Prison in Raleigh—which, ironically, was where she was originally supposed to be housed, serving her seven-to-ten-year sentence on the breaking and entering conviction. After that conviction, Little had asked to be held in Washington's jail, rather than the prison in Raleigh. She was appealing her conviction, and the location was more convenient—and, frankly, more comfortable. One wouldn't wander down the hall in state prison to make a phone call in the office or enjoy a cold soft drink.

While much of what happened that night wasn't in dispute, what happened in that cell during the critical time, only two people could report with certainty. One was dead. The other had reasons to escape and hide for her very life.

Even when she finally told her story, even when it was supported by the available physical evidence, some wondered which interpretation of the facts to believe—was she forced to perform a sex act against her will? Or did the twenty-year-old lure the sixty-two-year-old white jailer into a trap of his own vulnerability so she could escape?

The Nation Watches

The August events didn't really get national attention until months later, in December 1974, when *The New York Times* published an article on the case.

The case had everything that made it headline worthy—but the tenor of the headlines varied greatly, depending on who was writing and who would read them. In the South, the images, the fears, the embarrassment, the anger were too close to home. In the South, Black and white people lived close by each other, especially in small towns—maybe not right next door to each other, but close enough.

And southerners were sensitive about the perception outsiders had of them—perceptions that usually were not flattering. In April 1975, James Reston Jr., a writer living in Hillsborough, wrote a lengthy *New York Times Magazine* article on the case. He used a quote from David Milligan, editor of the local Beaufort weekly newspaper, to describe the "stereotyped picture the townspeople believe the nation is getting of their home."

> *This is the South. Here's a rinky-dink town with its shacks and shanties. You got this old redneck sheriff and this old redneck jailer and this pore little ole colored gal.*
>
> *She's there in jail, so defenseless, so innocent, and she gets raped and ravaged by this gross jailer, and all of a sudden, out of nowhere, she struck out, trying to defend herself. She had to kill the jailer, and now those ignorant old rednecks are gonna get their revenge on her. They're gonna make her pay for it with her life.*

Milligan said it wasn't enough to point to other parts of the country as more bigoted than Washington, North Carolina. Guilt couldn't be transferred or alleviated by pointing to someplace else worse off. *The New York Times Magazine* quoted Milligan: "We've got no responsibility for Boston or Harlem. We've got to see to it that things are right in our own town. The point is that Joan Little is here."

The Reverend Ralph Abernathy Sr., a powerful leader in Martin Luther King Jr.'s Southern Christian Leadership Conference, gave another perspective to *Jet* magazine: "I ask North Carolina, if there was a white woman who had stabbed a Black man who was attempting to rape her, would that white woman be on trial today? That white woman would be given a medal of honor. Well, hell, we think as much of our women as white men think of their women."

Little's defense attorney, known for antics inside and outside courtrooms that stirred supporters and antagonized judges, knew he had a landmark case as soon as he drove to Washington to take Joan Little to Raleigh and arrange her surrender. "I knew immediately that if I was to get Joan Little free, I'd have to do some things that you don't ordinarily do in a case. I had to get it out of Washington. I had to have money, and I had to create a big public interest. Without these three things, I'd never win it."

The Free Joan Little fund helped support a stellar list of defense attorneys and spent $30,000 hiring social scientists to poll the residents of Beaufort County to measure potential jurors' prejudice against Black people, women and young people.

In one of the first uses of social science to guide jury selection, the money raised by Free Joan provided jury pool research that convinced the judge to grant the change of venue and move the trial to Raleigh.

The trial started on July 14, 1975, and lasted five weeks. The jury needed only seventy-eight minutes to return their verdict: not guilty.

Joan Little was the first woman to be acquitted of murder for defending herself after a sexual assault.

Long after, some involved in the case continued to make headlines. Karen Galloway, a member of the defense team, was a newly sworn lawyer when Jerry Paul asked her to join them. She later became the first Black female judge in Durham County. Over a decade after the Little trial, after an ethics reprimand in another case, Paul was disbarred in 1987.

Joan Little was free for four months awaiting her appeal on the breaking and entering charge that put her in the Beaufort County Jail that August night; the court denied her appeal, and she was sent to Raleigh's women's prison to serve her sentence. After her release, she was arrested in New York for driving a stolen car. Afterward, she disappeared from public view.

When a case becomes bigger than just a case, when it becomes a platform or a cause célèbre or a rallying cry or a symbol, it becomes more difficult to understand the story. It becomes more complicated than just those involved and what happened to them. For Joan Little, her trial became bigger than itself—before it faded.

The Spy Who Came to Chapel Hill

In the Research Triangle, centered by Research Triangle Park (RTP) and three major research universities—the University of North Carolina at Chapel Hill, Duke University and North Carolina State University—one might not be surprised to learn of industrial espionage, illicit efforts to capture potentially lucrative information.

However, one might be surprised to learn that Chapel Hill attracted a spy of a different stripe—a genuine Cold War–era State Department official at the U.S. Embassy in Vienna who was suspected of being a Soviet KGB agent. Or was he really just delivering stamps, from one dedicated stamp collector to another, on the occasions when he met with a known KGB operative in Brussels and Paris?

The life and times of Felix Bloch were as fascinating as those created by spy-writing masters John le Carré and Ian Fleming. But fact and fiction differ in a key aspect—a good novelist lets the reader in on the secret, gives a glimpse behind the curtain. In the real world of international espionage, no one lifts the curtain to allow a peek if he knows what's good for him. So those standing outside trying to understand the intricate real-life stories are left with questions and few answers.

In 1992, customers at the University Mall Harris Teeter grocery in Chapel Hill might have had their eggs and cereal bagged by a tall, thin, dapper man with a fringe of close-trimmed hair circling his bald dome and sometimes wearing large metal-framed glasses. A few might have known his backstory. College towns, after all, collect and even celebrate folks who might not fit in elsewhere.

Bloch was a career diplomat, one who aspired to promotions that never quite came. With Bloch's experience, he could've expected to be a deputy chief of mission or even chief diplomat at a smaller embassy, one former boss said. Instead, Bloch was shipped home in 1987. The explanations his former superiors offered in public interviews ran the gamut. Former ambassador to Austria Ronald Lauder—son of cosmetics mogul Estée Lauder—said he fired Bloch, that Bloch was always going outside channels and was insubordinate. Bloch, for his part, considered Lauder the diplomatically tone-deaf son of a rich woman.

The director of the Foreign Service said Bloch wasn't fired, that Bloch was in line for promotions and it was time for him to rotate out of Vienna, so the director himself returned Bloch stateside.

As the varying public explanations illustrate, working in the Foreign Service was, by its nature, fraught with politics, even without the foreign intrigue. Some diplomats worked their way up through the service, while others were political appointees, often granted as thanks from a grateful president for their political fundraising and support. Infighting could naturally develop.

As a career diplomat in Vienna, Bloch brought certain skills. For one, he spent his childhood in Vienna. He spoke German with ease. He had degrees from the University of Pennsylvania and the University of California at Berkeley. He'd served posts in Singapore, Venezuela and Berlin.

The story shifts into spy thriller territory in May 1989. Bloch was surveilled by French counterintelligence agents when he met with Pierre Bart, a bearded, bear-sized man, in a hotel bar on the Rue de Rivoli in Paris. The two men drank whiskey at the bar and then had wine and dinner in the expensive Restaurant Le Meurice, with its Versailles-inspired gold-and-white décor.

After dinner, Bloch left a shoulder tote he'd carried from his hotel for Pierre Bart.

The details of their dinner wouldn't have been recounted in *The New York Times Magazine* a year after that meeting except for one key fact: Pierre Bart was a real-life Soviet agent, a Finn named Reino Gikman when he was in Vienna and Pierre Bart when he was in Paris.

After Bloch returned to the United States, he agreed to host an interview with journalist David Wise in his elegant Washington apartment—the only interview he gave. Bloch explained the tote bag contained stamp albums and sheets. He'd left them for Bart's consideration, a perfectly ordinary exchange of stamps between collectors. His story never varied over the years. Bloch had been an avid philatelist since he was young—and had his longtime collection and deep knowledge to prove it. Starting when he was first confronted with the surveillance photos of him and Bart/Gikman in the Paris restaurant, his answer had always been the same—he was contacted by someone he knew as Pierre Bart, a stamp collector. He took some stamps to Bart, as stamp collectors do with fellow collectors.

Journalist Wise succinctly summed the intrigue that swirled around Bloch: "The case had everything: A media and F.B.I. circus; an elusive K.G.B. agent with at least three identities who has vanished; his mistress, an attractive widow who lives behind barbed wire in Vienna, guarded by a pit bull; a blond Viennese prostitute specializing in whips and leather; and rumors of a spy ring operating from the Soviet UNESCO mission in Paris."

In 1990, the case was also remarkable because Bloch was the highest-ranking government official suspected of spying for the Soviets who was never charged or tried for any crimes. The Washington press followed Bloch around, along with what was surely an FBI surveillance team, for months. News photos showed him strolling calmly along with a gaggle of cameras and boom mikes surrounding him in a paparazzi parade. He couldn't sit on a bench and read a paper without being photographed. One photo, showing a group of video cameramen clustered behind him, was captioned "Bloch Party."

Unfortunately for those lugging large cameras and hoping the quiet man would say or do something worth recording, Felix Bloch was an inveterate walker. On one oft-reported day, he took his followers on a twenty-two-mile walk in the heat and humidity of a Washington August.

No one posited a clear reason for Bloch to become a KGB agent. He was no fan of communism and he had the advantage of family money—his father had been a successful paper exporter; his routine financial disclosure forms showed he had assets up to $1 million, and his thoroughly vetted bank accounts never showed any suspicious transfers.

Perhaps he was blackmailed? He did regularly hire the same prostitute in Vienna over his seven-year assignment there. He didn't get along with all his superiors, especially Lauder, whom he ridiculed when Lauder's mother called to check on security precautions for her son.

No one could suggest what documents might have been stolen or copied and given to Bart/Gikman.

So, Bloch retreated to Chapel Hill, building a modest house at the Governors Club, where his $220,000 home fit the requirement of a good investment—the cheapest home in the up-to-$1 million neighborhood.

Why settle in North Carolina? His wife grew up in Saluda, in the western North Carolina mountains. Her father had operated the Esso station and was once a state senator, so family might have been one reason. Plenty of other diplomats also retired to the area, though Bloch didn't seem to be much of a joiner.

However, he was always a workaholic. That might explain why, in 1992, he took jobs at the grocery store and as a part-time bus driver for Chapel Hill Transit, where workmates gave him good reviews.

Entrance to the exclusive Governor's Club in Chapel Hill where diplomat Felix Bloch lived. *Photo by Cathy Pickens.*

Nothing really explains his two shoplifting arrests in 1993 and 1994; one for $109 from the grocery store where he worked, which led to him being fired.

In 2001, Bloch was back in the news for reasons no crystal ball could have predicted. FBI special agent Robert Hanssen was arrested on February 18, 2001, in what was named the most damaging spy case in U.S. history.

Hanssen's one-hundred-page affidavit to the FBI was the first account from inside the Bureau about its investigation of Felix Bloch a decade earlier. Hanssen admitted to informing his KGB contacts about the FBI's suspicions of Bloch; the KGB in turn alerted Bloch, according to the FBI. Hanssen quoted a letter he sent the SVR (the KGB's successor): "Bloch was such a schnook....I almost hated protecting him, but then he was your friend."

Hanssen's affidavit went on to blame the FBI's cautiousness for not catching and convicting Bloch of treason. Had the agent sent to Paris been more decisive, Bloch and Gikman "would have been dead meat," Hanssen said.

The petty backbiting in the Foreign Service and the FBI sounded more like a bad comedy sketch than missives from the sanctified halls of high-ranking public servants. The revelations from Hanssen's arrest brought into public view what had stayed behind the scenes during the time journalists and agents tracked Bloch around Washington. In the end, after the dust settled, he remained a free man. The government lacked evidence to prosecute him.

In an interesting coda to the spy story, in 2003, the North Carolina Museum of History played host to the first Raleigh Spy Conference, billed as "Spies, Lies and Treason: The KGB in America." The secrecy inherent in the spy business makes gathering the pieces of the complicated stories almost impossible. *Indy Week* writer Jon Elliston, covering the event, reported some of those behind-the-scenes details presented at the conference by Brian Kelley. Kelley had once been suspected as the traitor—before Robert Hanssen was unmasked as the real mole.

In his job as a CIA counterintelligence expert, Kelley was the one who uncovered the contacts between Bart/Gikman and Bloch. When an unknown insider tipped off the KGB about the Bloch investigation, suspicions turned on Kelley as the mole, not on Hanssen. Until Hanssen was unmasked, Kelley's personal and professional life was turned upside down. Neither Kelley nor the conference organizer—publisher and spy lore enthusiast Bernie Reeves—had kind words for Felix Bloch. Both were convinced he'd gotten away with treason.

Elliston noticed the surprise guest in the spy conference audience: Andrea Bloch, Felix's daughter. She attended to take in what the experts said and try to process it. She'd first learned of the suspicions about her father when FBI agents showed up years earlier at the art gallery where she worked in New York City. She told Elliston about her reaction to their questions: "You start questioning everything—everything in my life, everything I knew, all my experiences, were suddenly up in the air."

For his part, Bloch never bothered to protest his innocence. "There's no way to prove you are innocent," he told seasoned spy journalist David Wise in 1990. "There's a presumption of innocence in this country. Someone should not be put in the position of saying 'I'm innocent.'" Was this part of his "remote, Teutonic persona," his "dark and nihilistic view of life" that Wise linked to his unwillingness to defend himself? In interviewing Bloch, Wise also "found a highly intelligent, even likable, but haunted man."

The North Carolina Museum of History in Raleigh, site of the 2003 conference on spies and spying. *Photo by Cathy Pickens.*

To understand a job—or life—of secrets, those seeking answers must put together the puzzle as best they can from the scattered evidence and multiple perspectives. In Bloch's case, those pieces never fell neatly into the picture his pursuers expected.

During the time Bloch was under heavy surveillance, the government bugged his Mercedes sedan. His wife later found the device. One news article reported he'd been overheard telling his wife he had received money from the Soviets. Bloch told journalist Wise that he actually told her he'd been *accused* of taking money—that's what was overheard.

At the spy conference, his daughter met David Major, who'd been assigned by the FBI to work the first stages of the Bloch investigation. He told her agents bugged the car, hoping Bloch would reveal something to his wife. The windows were down, so outside noise prevented them from hearing.

Some people are better at keeping secrets than others. And being suspicious must be an occupational requirement—or hazard—for a spy. Those on the outside can only speculate—and attend conferences hoping to gather the disparate parts of the story.

The last Raleigh Spy Conference was held in 2012.

PRISON BREAK

Seventy-five miles northwest of Raleigh, near the community of Blanch in Caswell County, sits what once was North Carolina's "Little Alcatraz."

Ivy Bluff had been built for one purpose: to house the worst of the worst, an impregnable fortress isolated near the Dan River. Built to hold only forty male prisoners, Ivy Bluff opened in 1956.

On December 9, 1959, huge headlines screamed: "20 Armed, Dangerous Convicts Flee State's Strongest Prison" and "Where Cons Got Hacksaw Is Puzzle to Officials."

A review of other U.S. prison breaks shows no other escape involving so many prisoners—and certainly no break where such a high percentage of the prison's inmates walked past the guard tower and out the gate together.

The day after the prison break, news reports identified the four masterminds. All of them were housed in the segregation unit in individual cells to limit their contact with other prisoners and, presumably, to limit their ability to plan mischief. The four were James Christy from Concord, Charles "Yank" Stewart from Wilmington, James Strickland from Columbia

Ivy Bluff Prison opened in 1956 to house the "worst of the worst," those Central Prison in Raleigh couldn't handle. *Photo by Cathy Pickens.*

and Douglas Anderson from Atlanta. Their sentences ranged from nineteen years (breaking and entering and armed robbery) to life (burglary and kidnapping). Their ages ranged from twenty-four to fifty-two.

Yank Stewart, the oldest man among the escapees and one of the masterminds, had a history of prison breaks. The crimes that sent Yank to various prisons were remarkably nonviolent: he robbed stores and stole cars. His ex-wife said he "wasn't a drunk." He didn't hurt people. But he didn't like being told what to do—which meant he really didn't like being in prison.

Some in his family thought any perception of Yank as a criminal had more to do with his father and his older brother, Elmer, than with Yank himself. Yank's father, C.W. Stewart, was a Wilmington-area bootlegger during Prohibition, a more lucrative career than fishing or farming in the 1920s. But when confronted in an armed raid on their moonshine still, C.W. and Elmer shot and killed a revenuer and a deputy U.S. marshal. Even though the jury recommended mercy, the two were executed in Raleigh's electric chair—making history as the only father/son duo to face that fate.

Yank wasn't stupid, though his rural upbringing might have let some underestimate him. He apparently did well in school, reaching a seventh-grade proficiency before he dropped out in the fourth grade. His IQ was recorded as 101, about average. But according to the *Charlotte Observer*, a state psychiatrist's report said, "Stewart makes a poor impression because of his low-class family background....It is evident from talking to him that he is somewhat bitter toward adversity, especially about the execution of his brother and father, though he has never showed a tendency towards revenge against any law enforcement officer or judge."

Though he "suffered from bad associations, poor education and low mentality," the evaluator noted that "he had leadership tendencies and is a schemer."

Yank seemed to be a live and let live kind of guy, stealing to support himself but not violent or vindictive. He was, though, quite proud of his ability to escape.

He tallied up at least six escapes. The one he seemed to most enjoy was in 1954, when he used a hospital visit as a ruse while in custody in Wilmington. Once outside the jail and on the way to the hospital, he drew a gun on the sheriff's deputies and took off. The gun he pulled was one he'd lovingly crafted from soap.

Perhaps Stewart borrowed the soap pistol idea from another famous prison escapee. In 1934, John Dillinger outwitted yet another "escape-proof" lockup, the county jail in Crown Point, Indiana. Despite being guarded by police and the National Guard, Dillinger's fake wooden gun, black and shiny with shoe polish, was his key to the door.

In a Thanksgiving interview less than two weeks before their Ivy Bluff escape, James Christy, another of the leaders, told a *Charlotte Observer* reporter, "They can't keep me here. I'm gonna leave one way or another."

During the breakout, Christy reportedly told a guard they'd been planning it for about a month, so announcing it to a reporter in the midst of planning it was indeed brazen.

Christy and Stewart admitted the guards didn't treat them roughly—with one exception, Stewart said. Stewart was hanging his hands through the door of his cell when a guard rapped his fingers with a broom and told him to keep his hands inside. That incident made Stewart angry—and gave him an idea. The next time he had the chance, he slammed his hand in the door, injuring himself badly enough to merit a trip to the infirmary at Central Prison.

Christy also got a trip to Central Prison for treatment after he burned his foot. Together, the two concocted a successful escape from the medical unit. They first sawed through the bars. Using a salve from the medical supplies, they dyed bed sheets purple so the white color wouldn't stand out against the bricks. They lowered themselves from an upper window and then used bunk bed ladders they'd taped together to scale a seven-foot wall and eluded capture for ten days. Yank was retaken at a gas station they were trying to rob in Summerfield in Guilford County. Christy ran to a nearby barn and was tracked by bloodhounds.

Until they made it over the wall, Central Prison hadn't seen an escape in a decade, and the two were just getting started. Their Raleigh escape was in October 1959, just weeks before they worked out their takeover and escape from the inescapable Ivy Bluff prison.

Aerial view of Central Prison in 1949. *Photo courtesy of Wikimedia Commons.*

For the Ivy Bluff escape, the *Charlotte Observer* reported the "desperadoes took advantage of guard carelessness to seize control of the entire prison and help themselves to an arsenal of weapons that included a sub-machine gun."

Only one escapee, a burglar from Gastonia serving a life sentence, had been recaptured by the time the newspapers went to press. A State Wildlife Commission plane had spotted him, and bloodhounds tracked him. Not surprisingly, headlines that day also said, "People Jittery in Ivy Bluff Area" and "Prisons Director Seeking Answers."

State Prisons director William F. Bailey gave reporters a detailed explanation the day after the escape, walking them through a guided tour of how it had taken place. At 9:15 p.m. on Monday, Yank Stewart had called to the guard covering the segregation unit. Stewart said he needed toilet paper. When the guard arrived with the paper, a prisoner farther down the hall yelled that he was the one who asked for the paper.

The guard moved to that cell, which took him farther from the unlocked hallway door. After the guard passed Stewart's cell, Stewart crawled out the eleven-inch-square opening he'd cut by sawing loose two three-quarter-inch bars at the bottom of his cell door. The other three masterminds crawled from similar holes in their doors.

Prisoners still locked in their cells grabbed the guard's feet and held him until Stewart and the others could overpower him. Had the guard followed protocol and locked the hallway door between Stewart's cell and the others, Stewart couldn't have jumped him from behind.

From there, it was a matter of lying in wait for the next guard, who carried keys to more doors, to come through on routine patrol.

As soon as Prisons Director Bailey arrived on the scene, he fired the first guard the prisoners overpowered. *Charlotte Observer* reporter Kays Gary said the guard's wife was in tears when she learned he'd been fired. "He was fixin' on getting a $7.50 raise," she said, "and we needed it bad. The baby here is sick. Now there's nothing."

The second guard fired on the spot was months away from retirement, dismissed for not checking the integrity of the bars on the cell doors on every shift, as spelled out in prison procedure. The guard told Kays Gary he was the only one who ever bothered to check the bars, and "it took a long time to saw those bars through," he said. He wasn't the only guard who could've uncovered the scheme.

How had they gotten the hacksaw? That question had a hint of an answer early on; an honor grade prisoner had been seen outside a window "fooling around" at some point. Likely he'd supplied the saw from a work shed to

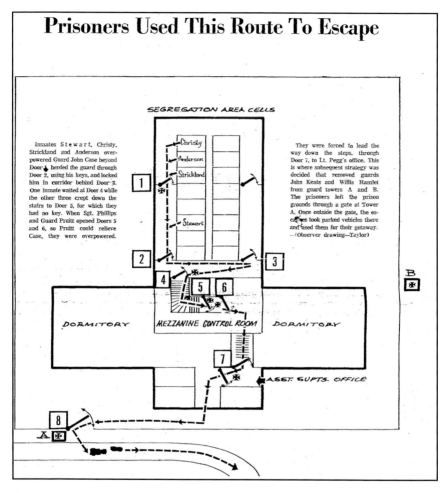

Prisoners Used This Route To Escape

SEGREGATION AREA CELLS

Inmates Stewart, Christy, Strickland and Anderson overpowered Guard John Case beyond Door 1, herded the guard through Door 2, using his keys, and locked him in corridor behind Door 3. One inmate waited at Door 4 while the other three crept down the stairs to Door 5, for which they had no key. When Sgt. Phillips and Guard Pruitt opened Doors 5 and 6, so Pruitt could relieve Case, they were overpowered.

They were forced to lead the way down the steps, through Door 7, to Lt. Pegg's office. This is where subsequent strategy was decided that removed guards John Keats and Willis Hamlet from guard towers A and B. The prisoners left the prison grounds through a gate at Tower A. Once outside the gate, the escapes took parked vehicles there and used them for their getaway.
—(Observer drawing—Taylor)

DORMITORY   MEZZANINE CONTROL ROOM   DORMITORY

ASST. SUPTS. OFFICE

Above: Map of the prisoners' escape route. *Map courtesy of Charlotte Observer and the Robinson-Spangler Carolina Room, Public Library of Charlotte-Mecklenburg County.*

Opposite: Ivy Bluff prison guard tower at time of the escape. *Photo courtesy of Charlotte Observer and the Robinson-Spangler Carolina Room, Public Library of Charlotte-Mecklenburg County.*

those in segregation. Even though guards could see the isolation unit cells, they observed no suspicious actions before the takeover.

A little after midnight, twenty of the thirty-seven prisoners in Ivy Bluff walked out the front gate of the prison. The two guard towers were empty. The guards were locked in cells on the segregation hall, and the prisoners had commandeered rifles, pistols and a submachine gun.

No one among the guards or prisoners, labeled North Carolina's worst, was injured or killed during the unprecedented and remarkably nonviolent escape—the largest prison escape in U.S. history.

In a 1993 interview with Jim Schlosser for the *Greensboro News & Record*, James Christy recounted Ivy Bluff among his many "great escapes." Despite being so much younger than Stewart—Christy was twenty-six at the time of his escapades with Stewart in 1959—he'd racked up his own record of escapes from prison camps all across the state.

In his interview at age sixty, he presented a surprising attitude toward crime, early 1990s-style. "Back in my time I would have hurt someone if I had to, but this [the 1990s] is outrageous. They shouldn't show them no mercy. Going into a convenience store and hurting someone, that's ridiculous."

Of one of his other escapes, he told Schlosser he "could have easily killed the guard he kidnapped when he hijacked the truck in Burnsville. Instead, he let the guard go and gave him back his lunch pail and jacket. 'I wished I hadn't because I near 'bout froze and starved to death that night hiding out in the mountains.'"

Guard tower and gates at abandoned Ivy Bluff/Blanch Correctional Institution. *Photo by Cathy Pickens.*

Yank Stewart was so famous that he earned a mention in a memorial article on the career of a North Carolina Highway Patrol trooper. C.L. Swartz died in 2012 at age eighty-five. An article about his exploits included mention that he'd once joined a high-speed chase to capture a bank robber (speeds up to 108 miles per hour, according to the report) while transporting a prisoner to trial in Elizabethtown. Trooper Swartz's other career highlight was arresting Yank Stewart after he pulled a gun and robbed a Wilmington grocery store.

Yank Stewart went on to spend more years of his life in prison and even served a stint in the real Alcatraz, taking in the view of San Francisco and painting landscapes, but he finished his days as a city gardener, caring for Wilmington's roses. He died in 1985 at age seventy-nine.

In 2017, North Carolina put the former Ivy Bluff prison up for sale. According to Raleigh reporter Josh Shaffer, over the years it had several reincarnations. First, the name changed to Blanch Correctional in 1963. (No prison official could feel good still calling it Ivy Bluff after all the escape headlines.) They added a second story in 1967 and a metal processing building in 1971 to supply stainless steel and iron for state use. For a while, it housed prisoners too sick for other facilities and then youth offenders before it closed in 1999. Asbestos and lead contamination were too expensive to abate.

The price set for the twenty-three acres and eighteen buildings was $152,000. According to records as of 2020, the property might still be available.

CAMPUS CRIMES

THE DUNGEONS & DRAGONS CASE

Every few years, a new cultural phenomenon appears that captivates teens and befuddles their parents. Ducktail haircuts and Elvis in the 1950s, flower power in the 1960s, followed by rap music, video games and countless other "threats" were heralded as the sure destruction of the younger generation, each in its turn. Through the 1980s, Dungeons & Dragons stepped into the spotlight of moral panic, in part because of a North Carolina homicide.

When D&D, as insiders termed it, caught headlines in connection with a violent murder in eastern North Carolina, it wasn't the first case associated with the fantasy role-playing game. It was yet more proof for those who warned that players who immerse themselves in fantasy quests for hours or days on end might get lost in them.

As often happens, fear over the game attracted attention to the murder. But the death of Leith Von Stein and the attack on his wife were frightening not because of a demonic D&D adventure game but because the tragedy happened in a normal, successful, small-town southern family.

The case began in the summer of 1988 with three friends, students who had just finished their freshman year at North Carolina State University. James Upchurch, Christopher Pritchard and Neil Henderson were smart, but they also liked to party.

Henderson and "Moog" Upchurch, also nicknamed "Bart," had known each other since they were kids in Caswell County, north of Raleigh toward

Greensboro. They had been selected to attend the same high school program for academically gifted students.

The two met Pritchard when he responded to a flyer posted around North Carolina State about joining a group to play Dungeons & Dragons.

According to Joe McGinniss's book detailing their crime, Upchurch served as their game's Dungeon Master, the one who laid out the adventures. Even in their casual exchanges, when they were out eating pizza, Upchurch would award "experience points" for challenges. On a typical night at Wildflour for pizza and beer, "Moog would shout, 'Five thousand experience points to anyone who beats on the table with his mug and yells, "Serving wench, bring us more ale!"' Moog would give them experience points for all sorts of things, such as stealing. The more expensive the object you stole, the more experience points you would get from the Dungeon Master. 'The whole point

North Carolina State Memorial Belltower in Raleigh. *Photo by Cathy Pickens.*

was, for doing something daring in real life, you'd be given points for your character. With the points, the character would accumulate wealth and power and advance to a higher level.'"

The three stayed on campus that summer, but instead of focusing on classes, they spent their time being teenage boys with some freedom and some spending money, doing drugs and playing D&D—sometimes with real weapons in NC State's underground steam tunnels. Unfortunately, the fun took its toll on their grades. Henderson, with his 1500 SAT score (of the maximum 1600), had already flunked out. Pritchard was worried about his stepfather's reaction to his poor grades.

Pritchard's mother, Bonnie, had been a single mother working and going to school when she met Leith Von Stein. At the time, they both worked at Integon in Winston-Salem as computer programmers. Tensions between stepchildren and a stepfather aren't uncommon, but Von Stein seemed a caring and generous dad to Pritchard and his younger sister, Angela. As with many families, though, perceptions from outside can differ greatly from those inside.

The Von Stein family settled in Washington, North Carolina—the same town that witnessed the Joan Little case. Called the Original Washington (because it was founded before Washington, D.C.) or Little Washington (though residents don't really like that name), the historic waterfront town sits where the Tar River joins the Pamlico River, about two hours west of the NC State campus.

The family moved when Leith Von Stein became an executive—the internal auditor—with textile manufacturer National Spinning Company, the area's largest employer.

The Von Steins' two-story house stood on Lawson Road, a quiet street lined with two-story colonials, rambling brick ranch-style homes and large lots.

Leith Von Stein's family had started the Camel City dry cleaners, which grew to several stores in the Winston-Salem area, so he had been raised with a strong work ethic. Given his upbringing and his own drive to succeed, he became frustrated with Chris's lack of drive and his refusal to live up to what had been identified in school as his stepson's gifted academic potential. The tensions between the two grew as Chris asserted his independence his first year away from home.

Chris Pritchard drove a restored vintage 1965 Mustang, a gift from his parents. For his college expenses, they also gave him what was, by most measures, a generous fifty-dollar weekly allowance. Von Stein thought the money evaporated too easily. He worried Pritchard was spending money on drugs—not that Von Stein didn't know what it was like to be a young man on campus smoking some pot. He'd done the same thing when he was younger. But grades weren't Pritchard's priority, and Von Stein was tired of financing his fun.

One of the enduring mysteries of this case was how even family and friends closest to the events had trouble understanding what happened, even after it was all tried and settled.

What ended in a violent, deadly attack started as an off-hand, half-joking conversation among college friends. At first, they were talking about game strategy—an important part of D&D's addictiveness, the endless strategizing. Then, according to Neal Henderson, Upchurch and Pritchard introduced a real-world element. They had a plan for getting Pritchard's inheritance early, and the plan begun in jest got more detailed and elaborate the more they played with the idea. With the money, they could buy a nice house in North Raleigh and live there together. Pritchard promised them both the sports car of their choosing—Upchurch wanted a Porsche, and Henderson preferred a Ferrari. And they'd get $50,000 each for helping.

Pritchard's stepfather had recently lost his parents in quick succession and received his inheritance from the Von Stein dry-cleaning business, around $1 million. Von Stein used $600,000 of his inheritance to fund a trust for Angela and Chris. With the rest, he was planning to enjoy his later years with Bonnie.

In a time when the median household income was $25,000 a year, the money sounded like a fortune to three college guys who just wanted to role-play and take drugs and not work too hard or be accountable to anyone. Chris decided his stepfather wasn't shelling out the windfall generously enough in his direction.

Bonnie's first husband—Pritchard's father—had abandoned them, leaving Bonnie to work and to further her own education while also taking care of two small children. The sense of abandonment and the financial struggles left a mark on Chris, one that the comparative ease of life with a new stepfather and a new life in Washington apparently never erased. Or was the real problem his drug use? Or the immersive role-playing game and its elements of questing and violence? Or friends who would fall in with a dangerously real fantasy? Or a combination of elements, all leading to a plot to hurry along his inheritance?

What began as seemingly casual musings entered the realm of reality as the summer passed. In July, Pritchard hatched a plan for starting an "accidental" house fire with a generous helping of gasoline and a broken fuse as a red herring. On July 24, the attentive son grilled hamburgers for his family—dosed with crushed over-the-counter sleeping pills. But Pritchard and Upchurch couldn't crack the fuse and abandoned plans for starting the fire while the Von Stein family slept soundly that night.

The next plan involved an intruder who would attack with a machete. But the Army-Navy surplus store that sold machetes was closed.

The day after the failed fire attempt, Pritchard went to Kmart and bought a hunting knife. It cost half his weekly allowance.

The plan this time was for Henderson to drive Pritchard's white Mustang to Lawson Road in Washington. Upchurch would enter the house and do the deed. Pritchard would stay in Raleigh to make sure he had an alibi.

Henderson said later he didn't really think any of it would happen. It was all talk, just "an elaborate joke," until Upchurch, carrying the knife and a baseball bat, got out of the car.

In the early hours of July 26, 1988, Bonnie and Leith Von Stein were attacked while they slept. Bonnie was beaten and stabbed, but afterward, as she floated in and out of lucid moments, she managed to find the phone and call 911. She suffered blood loss, a broken thumb and a stab wound to the chest that collapsed her lung.

Her husband, who slept in the bed next to her, was dead before the police and paramedics arrived. He too had been beaten and stabbed.

Angela, asleep in her bedroom, was not harmed. She had a fan and radio on and said she heard nothing and never awoke.

For Henderson, things got seriously real when Upchurch climbed back in the Mustang. Henderson remembered Upchurch's words: "I did it. I can't believe I did it. I never want to see that much blood again for the rest of my life."

According to Henderson, they stopped three times on the way back to campus in Raleigh. First, they stopped so Upchurch could change clothes, throwing the bloody ones in the trunk. They then looked for an isolated area and set fire to the clothes, the knife and the map. As they neared Raleigh, they stopped for fast food and decided to wash the mud off the car.

Back near Washington, a hog farmer just finishing a dark-of-morning loadout of hogs headed for market spotted a fire in the woods near the road. He was tired and headed home but turned to make sure the fire wouldn't get out of control. The low area surrounded by swamp seemed contained, so he drove on home without alerting anyone.

Later, when it became clear something serious happened in Washington that night, he recalled the fire and notified police.

The fire hadn't done its job. Police found clothing, a hunting knife and a singed hand-drawn map of the neighborhood around Lawson Road—a map with handwriting later matched to that of Chris Pritchard.

From the first hours on the scene, the investigators doubted this was a random robbery. From where the window was broken at the back door, it was hard to reach the doorknob; valuables were left untouched downstairs; homeowners asleep upstairs were attacked—nothing looked like a routine breaking and entering.

The investigation continued for almost a year. Despite suspicions, the hard evidence to prove what police suspected wasn't easy to develop. After all, a jury would take some convincing to believe that a handsome, bright college student planned the murder of his parents and that his equally bright friends might have helped.

The case broke almost a year after the crime, when Henderson agreed to a conversation with police at the off-campus Wendy's where he was working. They came asking how to find Upchurch, who had disappeared. Investigators sat with Henderson in a plastic booth, asking questions yet again. The detective, in an attempt to shake something loose in the unproductive interview, took a wild shot to shake Henderson: "We know *for a fact* that Chris Pritchard is involved!"

Henderson admitted later the comment shook him. How could they possibly know anything about Pritchard?

Then he surprised the investigators. He responded with a simple question: "What if I just gave them advice?"

Henderson, no longer able to dodge his guilt, confessed.

Pritchard also eventually confessed. Both pleaded guilty and testified against Upchurch, the only one whose case went to trial. Upchurch contended he'd been framed by Henderson and Pritchard, that he hadn't participated in the crime, that they'd done it and set him up.

Upchurch's version is the only one not on the official record. He never confessed. He didn't testify at his own trial. His attorneys were reluctant to put Upchurch on the stand; he always had a smirk or grin on his face that wouldn't play well in front of a jury. So, his story was never heard.

The accounts Henderson and Pritchard gave didn't mesh on all points. But they weren't at the scene—and the drugs were ever-present. They both, though, placed Upchurch in the house with the weapons. Alone. Henderson admitted he drove the getaway car, nothing more. Pritchard had plenty of reliable witnesses that he was in Raleigh that night.

Other suspicions swirled around the case almost from the beginning. Bonnie and Leith Von Stein hadn't been outgoing community members in Washington. Few people knew them well. Bonnie was emotionally reserved in public. Angela too was seen as removed and unemotional immediately after the murder. People speculated whether they had anything to do with Von Stein's death.

The rumors and suspicions persisted even after the legal proceedings settled the questions of guilt beyond a reasonable doubt.

Pritchard and Henderson pled guilty. Upchurch was convicted at his trial.

The unexpected twists in the case weren't over, though.

While out on bail and living with his mother in Winston-Salem before he was scheduled to go on trial, Pritchard was treated by a psychiatrist. The psychiatrist insisted to his attorneys that Pritchard needed to confess to his mother about his role. The attorneys said absolutely not. If Pritchard went to trial, she would have to testify as a victim and the only witness to that night. They didn't want her on the stand with the knowledge that could convict

Pritchard. What was in Pritchard's best interest? The answer depended on whether one was fighting for Pritchard's mental well-being or his life.

Only two weeks before she took the stand to testify in Upchurch's trial about the night she was attacked and her husband killed, Bonnie Von Stein learned from her son the details of his own involvement. Pritchard had pled guilty and now he could unburden himself and tell her the bleak truth.

During the sentencing phase of Upchurch's trial, Bonnie again testified, as a victim in the attack. She told the jurors she didn't believe in the death penalty and she didn't believe in it for James Upchurch.

Despite her statement, James "Moog" Upchurch was sentenced to death. After an appeal, the court upheld the verdict but gave Upchurch a life sentence.

Pritchard got a life sentence for second-degree murder, for aiding and abetting the assault. He was paroled in 2007. Henderson was paroled in 2000.

Questions continued in Washington after the perpetrators were caught and convicted. Bonnie Von Stein stood by her son, even lived with him in Winston-Salem while the legal proceedings unfolded. At first, she simply couldn't believe he'd had anything to do with it. Some thought that suspicious, but what mother could believe her son had planned to kill her and her husband—and maybe his own sister?

Bonnie had bigger concerns than gossip. After the guilty pleas and the trial, she had come to terms with the unthinkable. She believed that without the drugs, Pritchard wouldn't have been involved. In Chris's sentencing hearing, she told the judge, "Now I am going to stand by him and be there for him. I will love him as I've always loved him."

Bonnie made another decision few in her position would consider. She wanted someone to research the whole story. She didn't want money for the story, and she didn't want the right to edit what was told. She wanted the story—because she wanted to understand it herself. She wanted perspective.

She studied the work of true crime writers before asking her attorney, Wade Smith, to approach the writer she thought could investigate and best tell the story: Joe McGinniss, the journalist who wrote *Fatal Vision*, his account of the notorious Jeffrey MacDonald case. Smith had been one of MacDonald's attorneys.

At the same time, North Carolina reporter and true crime writer Jerry Bledsoe was interested in the case. He had recently published *Bitter Blood*, based on his award-winning Greensboro newspaper series about a familial multistate series of murders.

Rarely have two successful crime writers approached the same case at the same time. Detailed and dogged, North Carolina native Bledsoe had access

Dungeons & Dragons dice. *Image courtesy of CompLady on Pixabay.*

to the police investigators and those who'd worked the scene of the crime. But Bonnie Von Stein gave personal access to only McGinniss. Ultimately, Bledsoe's *Blood Games* and McGinniss's *Cruel Doubt* both explored the case in well-researched detail.

In the end, what effect did Dungeons & Dragons really have on what became known as the D&D Murders? Early in the case, investigators learned how much Chris Pritchard loved the game. They noted that, when they questioned him, Pritchard only became animated when talking about D&D. For students headed to college, finding a place and people to fit in with is an important part of the experience. For Pritchard, Henderson and Upchurch, the role-playing game provided that place. Did the game control them, as some suggested? The young men didn't claim that. Were they under the sway of the Dungeon Master? Not based on their own words. But D&D provided a convenient way for those outside to understand the inexplicable.

The Von Stein case came at the end of a series of difficult cases where D&D played a peripheral role. In 1979, college student James Dallas Egbert tried to poison himself and then disappeared. Egbert was a sixteen-year-old prodigy attending Michigan State University. His family hired high-profile private investigator William Dear, who learned Egbert and his friends played D&D in Michigan State's steam tunnels. Egbert suffered from mental health issues and later died by suicide. *Mazes and Monsters*, the movie drawn from a fictionalized account of the case, starred Tom Hanks as a character inspired by a game to commit murder.

In 1982, high school student Irving Lee Pulling fatally shot himself. His mother, convinced D&D caused his suicide, tried to sue the high school principal who'd put a curse on him while playing the game. She also tried to sue the game's publishing company. She founded BADD (Bothered About

Dungeons and Dragons) to draw attention to the dangers of the game, garnering support from conservative Christian groups concerned about the game's evil fantasy and violence.

The dangers of the game became talk show fodder. A 1985 segment on the news magazine *60 Minutes* pointed the finger at D&D as a cause of teen suicide, but failed to cite solid evidence, critics of the episode contended.

D&D next figured in a case in 1987, when Daniel Kasten, an avid D&D player, killed his adoptive parents. He was afraid they would disown him because he'd gotten poor grades in college.

The 1992 Von Stein trial was the last high-profile case to raise the name of Dungeons & Dragons as a cause for violent behavior. The 1976 game had been out long enough that many players had grown up and become productive citizens. As *BBC News Magazine* pointed out, the game had "positive attributes. It was based almost entirely on the imagination, D&D was social. No screens involved." Based on those elements, D&D countered the objections many parents developed about video games.

In fact, some point to D&D as an important stepping-stone in their upbringing and in their creative lives. Pulitzer Prize–winning author Junot Diaz told journalist Ethan Gilsdorf how the game helped him as a marginalized "immigrant boy growing up" in New Jersey: "We welfare kids could travel, have adventures, succeed, be powerful, triumph, fail and be in ways that would have been impossible in the larger real world."

Celebrating the game's fortieth anniversary, Gilsdorf listed other successful and once avid D&D players: writer George R.R. Martin, comedians Stephen Colbert and Robin Williams, *The Simpsons* creator Matt Groening, the *Atlantic* editor Scott Stossel and many others.

With books exploring the case, a trial and fears about a demonic, mind-controlling game, do we have any better answers about what happened to a seemingly happy, hardworking family? The role of the game remains an unanswered question.

GUILTY OR INNOCENT?

Because of its abundance of colleges and universities, the Triangle area deals with a commensurate share of violence involving coeds. As the sad statistics show, when a college student is the victim of a violent attack, the student is often female.

NC State's D.H. Hill Library, where Betsy Parks Rosenberg studied on the night she was attacked. *Photo by Cathy Pickens.*

On the morning of May 6, 1975, before the North Carolina State University campus came to life at dawn, a passerby found a young woman bludgeoned to death, lying near her car. Elizabeth Parks Rosenberg, age twenty-four and a part-time student, had been in the library studying for exams around midnight. She announced to friends that she'd found the best parking spot on campus, in an insurance company lot near the D.H. Hill Library.

As usual when on campus, she carried her books and a leather shoulder bag. Her bag, along with her credit cards and wallet, was missing when her body was found, pointing police toward robbery as the motive.

Based on the scene, the working theory of the crime was that an assailant snatched her purse and she fought back. Once she was knocked to the ground, the assailant picked up a weapon lying close at hand—a metal pipe with concrete stuck on one end. She was struck violently in the face and the abdomen. She bled to death. A simple, stupid, brutal crime.

Betsy, as she was known, was an accounting major working part-time at Rex Hospital. She was the oldest of three, a National Merit Scholarship recipient and a member of the National Honor Society.

Police conducted more than one hundred interviews in the days following her murder. This kind of case galvanizes authorities and the community, particularly in a college town. But no arrests were made.

In August 1981, six years after the murder, as another school year was set to begin, the Raleigh police chief announced a task force had been working on area cold cases. Two of the "Big 3" cases he identified involved college students. One was Betsy Rosenberg. The other was Helena Payton, stabbed in a stall in her dormitory bathroom in 1979. She attended St. Augustine's College (now University), also in Raleigh and one of the oldest historically Black colleges in the nation.

As a result of the task force's efforts, both cases were announced as solved. But almost as soon as the cases were closed, questions arose. Did authorities arrest the right men?

In December 1981, four months after the Big 3 work was made public, a man named Gary Goldman was indicted for Betsy Rosenberg's murder.

At the time he was indicted, Goldman was serving time in Georgia for the murder of a store clerk during a robbery; he'd been sentenced in 1976 for that crime.

Goldman's name surfaced when Raleigh police happened to travel to Georgia to question a fellow inmate whose name had surfaced as a person of interest in Rosenberg's murder. The inmate pointed them toward Gary Goldman. Goldman reportedly told his prison buddy, the "jailhouse snitch," that he and another man grabbed a woman's purse near a college campus in North Carolina. A man with her tried to stop them, according to the story the snitch told investigators, but then ran off. Goldman dragged her out of her car and beat her with a fence post or metal with cement attached.

As a result of the inmate's story, police began looking at Goldman. In 1975, when Rosenberg was attacked, Goldman was seventeen and lived near the NC State campus. The morning after the murder, Goldman visited Tracy Current, who was living at Haven House, a residential drug rehab facility. Tracy Current asked Goldman about scratches on his arm. She testified he said something like "he didn't hurt as bad as she did or she got worse." He also had cash and "what appeared to be a credit card," which she found noteworthy considering Goldman's usual circumstances.

Current said nothing about this exchange until police questioned her in 1981, after the announcement of the cold case task force.

At Goldman's North Carolina trial, Current told the jury about Goldman saying he snatched a woman's purse near the college campus and that he had to hurt her when she fought back.

After Goldman's conviction, his appellate case centered on his failure to have a speedy trial. Appeals, after all, can only raise questions of law, including errors in admission of evidence or failure to protect the defendant's Constitutional rights. The North Carolina Supreme Court found no error in his trial.

Goldman served the minimum time on his sentence in Georgia. In September 1990, he became a ward of North Carolina's Department of Public Safety.

In a 2019 interview with Amanda Lamb, crime writer and reporter for Raleigh's WRAL, Goldman said, "Early on, I felt like [the North Carolina conviction] would be overturned, and when it wasn't, I kind of felt that I was guilty of the one in Georgia and this is just karma, an extension of that. I really wasn't bitter about it."

The Innocence Project

In 1992, attorneys Barry Scheck and Peter Neufeld founded the Innocence Project at the Cardozo School of Law in New York City to work on innocence claims and, in particular, to use then-new DNA technology to exonerate those wrongly accused. The organization grew into the international Innocence Network and included the North Carolina Center on Actual Innocence, which began in 2000. The non-profit, led by Christine Mumma, worked with students at Campbell, Duke, Elon, North Carolina Central and University of North Carolina law schools to investigate claims of actual innocence.

In addition to that case-by-case investigative work, in 2006, Mumma and state supreme court chief justice I. Beverly Lake Jr. shepherded the state legislature's creation of the North Carolina Innocence Inquiry Commission. The first of its kind in the country, the independent, state-funded commission reviews claims of actual innocence for serious crimes. When their review finds that a case merits judicial attention, the case is referred to a three-judge panel. Over a decade, the Innocence Inquiry Commission has reviewed roughly 2,800 claims, held 16 hearings and obtained 12 exonerations.

The commission and others passionate about equitable criminal justice want a system where the public can be confident in fair, reliable outcomes. Thanks to their work, North Carolina was the first state in the nation to standardize procedures for identification lineups—to avoid bias and use the best research in the field of witness identification—and one of the first to require that interrogations be recorded.

Christine Mumma became interested in Gary Goldman's case because she feared it had investigative flaws similar to those that plagued one of the other Big 3 cases on the 1981 Raleigh cold cases task force list—Helena Payton's murder at St. Augustine's College. The problems uncovered in James Blackmon's conviction for that murder might also have tainted Goldman's trial in Betsy Rosenberg's case. Both investigations were under pressure from the Raleigh police chief, who had provided travel budgets and support to bear down on solving the murders. The same detective worked both cases.

James Blackmon

Convicting someone for Helena Payton's murder didn't move as quickly as Goldman's conviction in Betsy Rosenberg's case did. In 1988, seven years after the Raleigh police chief named Payton's case one of the Big 3 cold cases he wanted solved, they got a guilty plea from James Blackmon for stabbing her to death in her St. Augustine dorm.

As early as 1983, almost two years after the task force started digging, police got a tip from an informant who pointed them toward a Raleigh mental hospital patient who claimed he'd killed women.

When task force investigators questioned Blackmon, he admitted to stabbing Helena Payton. They took him to the hall bathroom at the dorm, and he described what happened.

Rather than face a trial, Blackmon entered an Alford plea. In making an Alford plea, he didn't have to admit guilt. He only affirmed the police had enough evidence to convict him. The plea is usually made to avoid a harsher penalty if a jury finds the defendant guilty.

Entrance to the historic St. Augustine's University campus. *Photo by Cathy Pickens.*

For more than thirty years, Blackmon served his sentence. Even though Blackmon spent time in a mental hospital and even though he sometimes wore a Superman-style cape or claimed to be like Dracula or said he could cause earthquakes, the Wake County court in 1988 had declared Blackmon competent to stand trial.

Others disagreed.

In 2012, the Innocence Commission began investigating after Blackmon's case was referred by North Carolina Prisoner Legal Services. The investigation found detectives had played on Blackmon's mental illness by leading him to blame a "bad James" for the crime. No physical evidence linked him to the scene, and he was in New York at the time of the murder. Blackmon was convicted by only his own words, with no physical evidence or independent corroboration.

In November 2018, the Innocence Inquiry Commission referred Blackmon's case to a three-judge panel, the final step in the state's process. The three-judge panel "unanimously concluded that Mr. Blackmon has proven by clear and convincing evidence that he was innocent of second-degree murder."

In August 2019, James Blackmon was exonerated after more than thirty years. Helena Payton's murder was still unsolved.

Gary Goldman

Jean Parks, Betsy Parks Rosenberg's younger sister, often talked of her big sister's humor and how losing her changed their family gatherings. Despite her grief, she had been a vocal opponent of the death penalty. In a 2015 newspaper opinion piece, she presented a seldom-broadcast view from a victim's family member, one of compassion. She wrote about hearing a corrections officer who, twenty years earlier, described the preparations and procedures for execution by lethal injection. She said she thought about the family and friends of the condemned. "I imagined fear, anger, grief and powerlessness, the same overwhelming emotions I felt when Betsy was killed." Of her sister's case, she wrote, "When his life sentence was pronounced, I realized any healing I might experience depended more on what I did than on what happened to him."

Parks didn't just talk about reconciliation. She lived it. As a practicing psychologist, she served as a board member for Murder Victims' Families for Reconciliation. And she was instrumental in the two homicide support groups listed on the state website, in Buncombe and Wake Counties. (See https://www.nc-van.org/homicide-support-groups.) She knew the pain of loss—and she empathized with the pain of others, whether family members of victims or of those convicted in their deaths.

Journalist Sam DeGrave wrote about the Asheville–Buncombe Homicide Survivor Support Group. "Parks watched the trial and said that if she'd been on the jury, she doesn't know whether she'd have convicted the man accused of killing her sister, showing how muddy these court cases can be and how little they can do for the healing process."

Gary Goldman became eligible for parole. Christine Mumma, with her doubts about the investigations into the Big 3 cold cases, began working toward his parole hearing. In 2013, Mumma visited key witness Tracy Current.

Current was upset at first by the questions; she said she was supposed to be an anonymous witness. She made an interesting statement, though, when Mumma explained that she was looking for evidence to free Goldman. According to reporter Josh Shaffer, "Mumma said the former witness told her: 'That is what I've been praying for, I've been praying for him to find the truth. But I can't help you.'"

Two key witnesses pointed to Goldman at his trial: Current and the Georgia inmate. Current testified about Goldman's visit to her rehab facility on the morning after the murder. The inmate (who was investigators' initial target) said Goldman told him about snatching a girl's purse and beating her and about a man with her who fled, though no one else ever mentioned a man with Betsy Rosenberg that night. That was the entirety of the evidence against Goldman.

Gary Goldman was paroled in May 2019, almost two decades after he first became eligible for parole and after more than forty years in prison. He had served his time. But his release did not mean he was exonerated—despite his consistent claims of innocence.

After his release, Rosenberg's sister Jean Parks made an unusual request—she asked to meet Gary Goldman.

Goldman agreed. Christine Mumma facilitated the meeting.

In September 2019, at Campbell University's Raleigh campus, more than forty years since her sister's murder and thirty-six years since she'd first seen the man convicted of killing Betsy Rosenberg in a courtroom, Jean Parks sat down with Gary Goldman.

Parks's support of his parole played no small part in gaining his freedom.

Reporter Josh Shaffer covered the meeting for the *Raleigh News & Observer*. As she had watched the trial unfold, Parks had doubts about Goldman's guilt—despite the testimony against him, despite his failure to protest his innocence and his refusal to testify himself, Parks had doubts.

Adding to her uncertainty about his guilt, Goldman told her, "The first time he ever saw Current was the day she took the witness stand against him."

Campbell University Law School campus in Raleigh, where Jean Parks and Gary Goldman met. *Photo by Cathy Pickens.*

With that conference room meeting, Parks's "doubts about his guilt changed to near certainty of his innocence."

"I never did hate you, even when I thought you were guilty," she told her sister's convicted murderer. "I feel like we both got screwed by the same person…and by the system that failed to find the actual killer. And that feels like a bond."

Betsy Parks Rosenberg's murder remained unsolved. Mumma remained convinced Goldman wasn't the man who did it, and the Center on Actual Innocence continued to investigate.

TOO CLOSE TO HOME

ROBERT PETRICK

Having once known the pleasure of a close, loving relationship, finding love again would be a confident hope.

Janine Sutphen had had a loving marriage. She and her husband lived in Vermont and raised their three boys. She taught high school science, enjoyed playing her cello and loved to cook. She always maintained a welcoming, wide-open house full of children and friends. She and husband, Chazz, had entered the time of life when they could rightly expect to grow old and comfortable together—until he died in 1995 of heart disease, leaving Janine to reassess her life.

Her sons described her as "unconventional" and "a force of nature." After her husband's death, she decided to leave Vermont and build a new life in Durham, where she already had some friends. She joined the Durham Symphony Orchestra and continued to play her cello (though she never liked parking in the deck across the street where the musicians parked during rehearsals and performances). She took up belly dancing and weaving—"looming," her son called it. She continued her energetic, involved life.

But Janine missed the companionship of a man in her life. In 1999, she met Robert Petrick at church—a good place to meet a midwestern fellow—a computer consultant who shared her love of music and cooking. They were a good match, her sons and friends said. Janine and Robert married in 2001.

Historic Carolina Theatre, where the Durham symphony performed. *Photo by Cathy Pickens.*

In December 2002, Janine and her best friend, Margaret "Peg" Lewis, had breakfast together. Janine talked about the new job she would soon be starting, so Peg wasn't surprised when she didn't hear from Janine over the next several weeks. A new job, just at the holiday season, was a sure distraction.

Peg was surprised, though, when Rob Petrick left a message on her answering machine on January 22, 2003: "I'm trying to find out if you heard from Janine. I'm gonna call the police I guess."

Parking garage near Carolina Theatre, where Janine Sutphen's abandoned car was found. *Photo by Cathy Pickens.*

Petrick also called around to other friends and to Janine's sons. Janine had gone to symphony practice the night before but hadn't returned.

Peg Lewis had a bad feeling.

Petrick called the Durham police to report her missing. Not coming home or being in contact just wasn't like her. Petrick and her friends were understandably concerned.

Janine's car was found in the parking garage where she parked for symphony practice—the garage in a downtown business district at night, with few people around, where she'd never felt completely safe. Gang tags decorated parts of the area. Her car was in the lower level, a spot not as well-lit as the one where she usually parked, but no one knew what that change in her routine might mean. Police found no sign of struggle or violence in or around her car.

Her family and friends plastered the downtown streets with "missing" flyers. News reports across the region carried the story of the vanished cellist.

As weeks melted from late January into spring, no word or sighting of Janine came—until two men decided to go fishing. Falls Lake is a large recreation area in Wake, Durham and Granville Counties, at the head of the Neuse River. From their boat, the fishermen caught sight of something floating in the lake: the body of Janine Sutphen, wrapped in a sleeping bag inside a tarp. The tarp was circled with duct tape, with chains wrapped around the feet.

Far-Reaching Investigation

Despite the passing weeks, as hope that she would be found alive had begun to wane, police had not put their investigation on pause. They did what investigators usually do: they first checked out the missing woman's husband.

What they found was a trail of financial misdealings in Rob Petrick's past, and all involved taking money from women with whom he was romantically involved. They also learned that money was missing from the couple's accounts, money Janine likely hadn't known was disappearing. Or had she discovered it? Had she confronted her husband? At trial, Janine's friends testified she'd recently been afraid she didn't have enough money for groceries. One friend said she'd worried about losing her house and car.

Meanwhile, in Atlanta, Ann Johnston searched the online news reports with interest. Her fiancé had a friend named Janine who was missing in North Carolina and he was concerned.

Johnston and her fiancé had attended high school together before they went their separate ways for a few decades. In 2001, she reached out to him online and they renewed their high school acquaintance. Good timing for them, they were both single. He lived in North Carolina. They met in person and then a long-distance relationship blossomed. He gave her an engagement ring.

As Johnston read about the missing friend, she was blindsided. Robert Petrick? Was that the picture of her fiancé being arrested? He was married? To the missing "friend"?

Johnston and Petrick had been together for almost a year. Unbeknownst to Johnston, their relationship had started shortly after Petrick married Janine.

Johnston later told *Dateline*, "I knew right away that nobody knew anything about me." She called the Durham police.

Investigators added Johnston's story to the evidence they had accumulated about Petrick's history as a serial cheater, about his history of financial peccadilloes involving women in his life and about the couple's serious financial situation. As soon as Janine's body was identified, investigators moved quickly. They arrested Petrick on May 30, 2003, four months after he reported Janine missing.

The autopsy showed Janine had died from asphyxia, either from strangulation or from smothering. Petrick was indicted on murder charges and as a habitual felon; he had three prior felony convictions in Illinois. The court appointed Mark Edwards to represent him.

Two years later, in the months before his trial, Petrick fired Edwards and decided to represent himself *pro se*, without counsel. Despite no legal training, Petrick got to work while in prison, petitioning for access to the law library and preparing his case.

Proceeding *pro se* is a defendant's right. Any citizen is allowed to serve as his own counsel. Lawyers, of course, have a saying: Any lawyer who represents himself has a fool for a client. But in other, higher profile cases, criminal defendants have opted to represent themselves—Ted Bundy and Charles Manson, to name two. A *New York Times* article summarized the typical motives for *pro se* defendants:

> *Some criminal defendants who act as their own lawyers want a stage to promote an ideology; some apparently want the spotlight or think they can fare better than a real lawyer; some are too controlling to let anyone else be in charge; some are too paranoid to trust lawyers; and some are just delusional.*
>
> *Whatever the motive, it rarely ends well for the defendant. Judges routinely advise against it, and often insist that court-appointed counsel be on hand as a backup.*

Ego? A sense of superiority about his own intellect? Whatever the motive, Petrick was certainly not stupid. He even earned compliments from his court-appointed attorney for his skills.

The month-long trial began on Halloween 2005. Judge Orlando Hudson, who among his headline cases handled the Michael Peterson trial, Faith Hedgepeth's records hearings and ordered Floyd Brown released from the mental hospital for insufficient evidence, conducted the Petrick proceedings. He also, despite Petrick's move to represent himself, ordered Edwards to continue to be available as standby counsel.

A close friend testified Janine had called her at work, crying and scared. Janine had confronted Petrick once about their financial problems, and he choked her. Another friend testified that Janine confessed Petrick used a Taser on her in an argument over money. Another said he'd scared her when he tackled her and pinned her.

Her friends also helped build a timeline around her disappearance that directed suspicion at Petrick. Friends who regularly spoke with Janine said they hadn't heard from her or been able to reach her starting around January 5, 2003. Petrick told some, including her sons, she was sick, depressed, asleep or otherwise unable to come to the phone.

Petrick also claimed he too had been sick, unable to get out of bed to answer some of her sons' calls. At trial, though, the story unfolded that while he was reportedly confined to bed, he'd spent several hours one evening chatting up a woman at the James Joyce Irish Pub. He told her his wife died of cancer, gave her his email address and asked her to be in touch.

In representing himself, Petrick got to confront his former lovers, those he'd swindled, Janine's family and friends, the woman from Atlanta with his engagement ring. What had it felt like to sit in the witness box and be cross-examined by the defendant? Those face-to-face encounters in front of a courtroom full of media and court watchers couldn't have been easy for any of those who knew Janine or who had ever encountered Petrick.

When cross-examining the women, he got them to admit a key point: yes, he'd taken money, but he'd never been violent. He'd never been physically abusive. Even Janine's friends said they hadn't *seen* any signs of violence or abuse—only conversations where Janine reported she was scared, where he'd done something to hurt her. And no one could testify about the 2008 report showing a woman faces significantly increased odds of dying at the hands of her partner if he'd ever once put his hands around her throat and threatened to strangle her—that report had yet to be published.

In a word, the witnesses had to admit to a crowd of strangers that they had been gullible, preyed upon, swindled.

In tech circles reaching beyond the Triangle, the case earned the nickname the "Google murder." Forensic evaluation of computers seized from the couple's home showed alarming searches as early as late October 2002 (more than two months before Janine was likely killed). Investigators found searches about "Neck, Snap, Break and Hold" and bloodfest666. com's "22 Ways to Kill a Man with Your Bare Hands," which included a demonstration of a choke hold.

Searches done on January 8, around the time Janine was last seen, covered decomposition, the famous Body Farm research facility at the University of Tennessee, forensic entomology and rigor mortis.

On January 13, someone used the home computer to search for depth charts and boat ramps at Falls Lake west of Durham.

One of many remote boat ramps at Falls Lake near Durham. *Photo by Cathy Pickens.*

In his opening statement, Petrick admitted that evidence would show he'd been a serial cheater and a swindler. But that didn't make him a killer. Evidence suggested otherwise.

Investigators believed a key piece of evidence pointing at Petrick came from a cadaver dog. The dog, trained to signal its handler when it encountered the odor of decomposition, hit on the shower in Petrick's house and on the trunk of Petrick's car.

No witnesses saw him carry her body from the house. No one explained how he could fit her body, bound in the tarp, into the tiny trunk of his Miata. No one saw him dump the body into Falls Lake. Petrick made sure to emphasize those points.

At trial and on appeal, he challenged the validity of the cadaver dog evidence. He pointed out that crime scene specialists thoroughly searched his bathroom, including the drain traps in the shower, and found no blood evidence. How, he asked, could the cadaver dog find something when humans couldn't?

On cross-examination, the dog's trainer answered: "I can say that probably the forensics person couldn't—he don't have the nose the dog has."

The jury found Petrick guilty of first-degree murder; he was sentenced to life without parole.

Appealing his conviction, his first bone of contention was that the judge had allowed him to represent himself. The appeals court held that Judge Orlando Hudson, one of North Carolina's most seasoned trial judges, had properly cautioned Petrick against doing that.

Petrick also claimed the court shouldn't have admitted the cadaver dog evidence or statements that he'd attacked his wife or their financial problems or his past crimes. The appellate judges disagreed and upheld the guilty verdict. The court cited a U.S. Supreme Court case holding a "defendant who elects to represent himself cannot thereafter complain that the quality of his own defense amounted to a denial of 'effective assistance of counsel.'"

Following the failure of his appeals in state court, in a subtle but telling petition in his lengthy federal appeal, Petrick said Judge Hudson had failed to tell him that if he and his trial attorney "were at an absolute impasse as to trial decision, it would be [Petrick's] decisions that controlled." Petrick said, had he known he was in charge of the decisions about his defense, he wouldn't have fired his attorney.

The federal appeals court politely but firmly pointed out Petrick was mistaken. An attorney has a duty to consult with his or her client and to keep the client informed—not a duty to kowtow to a client convinced he knows more than the attorney. The court said, "The United States Supreme Court's well-known description of an attorney's responsibilities does not endorse the view that an attorney must capitulate to a client's preferences about the handling of a defense."

Petrick's conduct of his trial showed one consistent theme: he thought he was the smartest guy in the room. He also had a gift common to con men. As one of the jurors said in an interview with *Dateline*, Petrick's secret was he could read people. "They were all successful ladies." They weren't stupid; they were duped.

Petrick certainly wasn't North Carolina's only lonely-hearts swindler. Whether someone is looking for love for the first time or knows real love is possible because they've found it before, men and women—smart, successful people—can fall prey to those with no scruples about taking what they want.

The real mystery here is what changed in this relationship? Why kill Janine Sutphen? Why not walk away, as he'd always done before? He already had another lady lined up, waiting for him in Atlanta—the lucky one who found out in time. He knew how to convince them or leave—until, with Janine Sutphen, something changed. But what? To her family and friends, that question without an answer left a hole in their lives.

Mail Bomb

On July 11, 1995, headlines around North Carolina announced, *Bomb Explodes in Raleigh.* A mail bomb "rocked" the fifth floor of the nine-floor building across Six Forks Road from North Hills Mall. Two women in an office at BTI, a long-distance telecommunications company based in Raleigh, were injured. Five hundred employees of BTI and other companies in the building were immediately evacuated.

Initial reports said Tracy Bullis, a thirty-five-year-old manager and mother, had opened a package addressed to her. The blast severely injured her and blew a hole in the wall near the company mailroom. Her colleague Judith Harrison was also injured but was soon released from the hospital.

The two were longtime employees of the company. Bullis managed the leasing department arranging for transmitting BTI's long-distance service over local phone company lines.

BTI was the twelfth-largest long-distance phone provider in a crowded field of telecommunications companies in the United States. The Raleigh

Busy intersection of Lassiter Mill Road and Six Forks Road, near bombing site. *Photo by Cathy Pickens.*

office employed three hundred people. Tony Copeland, a BTI vice-president, described the women as "the icons in the company. They know everything. I have to go to them to find out things."

The company had received no bomb threats. In his initial interview with the press, Copeland wouldn't speculate about motives. "An incident like this is national," he said. "If it can happen at BTI, it can happen anywhere."

Random bombings had been in the news—spread across the country, some deadly. By 1995, the unknown University and Airline Bomber (which the FBI abbreviated to its case name UNABOM) had operated with impunity for almost twenty years. Starting in Chicago in May 1978, he'd planted bombs in offices, on an airline, in the parking lots outside computer stores and sent them through the mail, seemingly at random.

In the Raleigh case, news reports addressed the question that naturally came to mind as soon as this bombing became public: Was it the Unabomber? Police and FBI quickly announced they had no evidence the mysterious Unabomber was involved in the BTI bombing.

FBI special agent George Grotz in San Francisco, the spokesperson for the nationwide UNABOMB task force, emphasized they were investigating, but "at this point it does not appear to be the work of the Unabomber."

For the FBI, housing the task force in San Francisco made sense; San Francisco had significant experience with bombs and bombers of all types, based on the stunning number of bombing cases that particular office had handled in recent years. "Protest bombings were commonplace, with radical groups like the New World Liberation Front, the Red Guerilla Family, the Emiliano Zapata Unit, the Symbionese Liberation Army (SLA) and the Weather Underground operating with alarming frequency," according to journalist Lis Wiehl. "Bomb techs could barely finish processing evidence at one crime scene when they got word of another attack somewhere else in the city that needed their attention."

The devastation of large-scale, deadly domestic terrorist bombings put the entire nation on edge. Only months before the BTI bomb, in April 1995, the United States watched the aftermath of the tragic bombing of the Oklahoma City Federal Building and its 168 deaths, including 19 children.

Two years before that, in February 1993, terrorists parked a truck in the garage underneath New York's World Trade Center. The 1,200-pound bomb detonated, killing six people and injuring more than one thousand others. The building took hours to evacuate, and the crater reached several stories underground.

Nobody needed to be reminded of those bombings or the devastation and the fear they caused. As news of what happened on Six Forks Road in North Raleigh spread, everyone knew bombs were faceless, damaging and easily repeated.

Though not public knowledge until years after the BTI bombing, federal investigators had already studied the components in sixteen UNABOM devices and their aftermath. In those attacks, his bombs killed three people and injured twenty-three other victims—some severely and permanently. By the July 1995 blast in Raleigh, a look around the scene could tell them whether the device showed signs the Unabomber created it.

In 1987, almost ten years after he started, someone saw the Unabomber place a bomb for the first and only time. The box looked like a piece of debris sitting behind an employee's car tire in a parking lot outside a family-owned computer store in Salt Lake City. Another employee moved it aside so the driver could back out without hitting it and maybe damaging her car; it detonated and seriously injured him when he shifted it.

A witness saw the man leave the device behind the car and thought his behavior odd. As he stood to leave, the witness locked eyes with him. She helped legendary sketch artist Jeanne Boylan construct the famous hoodie-and-sunglasses sketch.

Portrait artist Boylan had worked over seven thousand cases and was known for her patient interviews with witnesses, which helped her pull from them a more complete portrait rather than the mechanical bits and pieces of an Identi-Kit reconstruction.

Jeanne Boylan's sketch from the only known sighting of the Unabomber. *Image courtesy of Wikimedia Commons.*

After the sketch was made public, the bomber went quiet, leaving no more bombs for six years. Had it been accurate enough to scare him off? The silence was so sudden and complete that some in the FBI hierarchy pushed for dismantling the multi-agency task force and returning the investigation to the local sheriff's office where the one death had occurred.

Investigators working the case argued that dismantling the task force would be dangerous. It had taken years to gather experts from the FBI, the ATF (Alcohol, Tobacco and Firearms) and U.S. Postal inspectors to bring their expertise to cases spread over so many jurisdictions. They now had systems in place to coordinate multiple law enforcement agencies. They had experts who'd studied the bomber's meticulous craftsmanship and could recognize it. The bomber was so cautious that he'd never left a useful serial number, traceable component, smudge of DNA or fingerprint. If he should start up again—and they doubted he would stay quiet forever—they would lose valuable time trying to pull resources and expertise together again.

That expertise allowed agents to quickly decide the Unabomber hadn't mailed or delivered the package to BTI in Raleigh, despite its association with a technology company—a prime target for the Unabomber. Sometimes knowing who didn't commit a crime can be a valuable investigative time saver. Ruling out the Unabomber as a potential suspect kept Raleigh investigators from chasing in the wrong direction.

While attention understandably focused on the country's most notorious, most mysterious and longest active bomber, police statistics pointed to other possibilities. Most workplace bombings are not from faceless terrorists with murky agendas. Most result from either a disgruntled employee, perhaps recently fired, who wants to exact revenge on his former employer and coworkers or a domestic dispute that erupts at the victim's workplace, perhaps because the angry spouse wants to draw suspicion away from the family home and the logical suspect who lives there.

The U.S. Postal inspector in Charlotte told reporters that North Carolina hadn't seen a letter bomb in years. For a decade, the United States averaged about sixteen letter bombs per year nationwide. Fortunately for the recipients, bombs are not easy to construct and do not work reliably. Two-thirds of those received fail to explode. In fact, 1995 remained a high-water mark for mail bomb injuries (eight) and deaths (two) nationwide, out of twenty incidents, until 2004, with twenty-six incidents, four injuries and no deaths nationwide. In other words, mail bombs were very rare and rarely deadly.

But bombs—and those who send them—are serious threats. Investigators mobilized quickly in Raleigh. In less than a week, Stephan Bullis, husband of the most severely injured victim, was arrested and charged. The Bullises had been married for five years, had one child together and lived in a quiet cul-de-sac near Knightdale. Newspapers reported Tracy Bullis's life insurance had recently been increased.

Bullis's lawyer, Joseph Cheshire, one of the most recognizable names among Raleigh defense attorneys, said Bullis was surprised by his arrest. "He felt like he had been very cooperative," Cheshire said, noting that Bullis even allowed police to search his home more than once.

Police had also kept him under careful surveillance as he drove back and forth between his home and Wake Medical to visit Tracy. After her release from the hospital, police escorted Tracy to her house to pick up clothing. They protected her and made sure she and her two children were in a safe place before Bullis's Saturday morning arrest in his lawyer's office in downtown Raleigh.

The Bullises' neighbors in the Beachwood subdivision were surprised. Stephan Bullis was a good neighbor, a founding member of the homeowners' association and its treasurer. He was a nice guy. Seeing him as a bomber out to injure or kill his wife wasn't a picture they could easily imagine.

In February 1996, seven months after his arrest, Bullis was found guilty in federal court. At trial, evidence was introduced that Bullis also sent a second bomb to her office building, but it wasn't delivered.

Tracy sat with her coworker Judith Harrison, listening to the verdict. The Associated Press reporter who observed the trial said she smiled before she began to cry. She had lost fingers and the thumb on her left hand.

Bullis received a life sentence in federal prison, which does not provide for parole. He never publicly gave a motive for the attack.

Though those small, deadly bombs delivered through the mail or left on the doorstep don't generate massive headlines beyond the local footprint of their impact, they are a persistent, anonymous, faceless, violent crime done at a distance—a crime that happens rarely but more often than most realize.

National headlines are reserved for the big bombings and the bombers who successfully evade capture for years. At the time of the Raleigh bombing, the then-unidentified Unabomber had offered to stop sending bombs if a national newspaper would publish his now-famous "Manifesto." After much negotiation, the manifesto was published on September 19, 1995. Because family members recognized key statements and style mannerisms in his writing, Ted Kaczynski was captured at his tiny Montana cabin a little more than six months later.

POLITICAL CONNECTIONS

Nation Hahn was just starting high school and Jonathan Broyhill had just graduated when they met at church summer camp. The friendship continued in their hometown of Lenoir, North Carolina, where they attended prayer group at a Pentecostal church and hung out at a local waffle shop. Friendships like theirs, formed during that growing-up time, can form lifelong bonds. In the case of Hahn and Broyhill, their friendship and their future were cut short in a vicious knife attack. But the friends couldn't see that coming.

After high school, Nation headed to the University of North Carolina in Chapel Hill, where he was a dedicated member of the Young Democrats. As a full-time student, Nation also worked full time for then-senator John Edwards's presidential campaign. While working on the campaign, he met energetic, politically passionate Jamie Hahn.

Jamie and Nation married in April 2009, with Broyhill serving as best man. Broyhill and Hahn maintained their close friendship even after Hahn left for college and Broyhill stayed in Lenoir to work at Lowes Foods.

The Hahns settled in Raleigh, where Jamie started her own firm, Sky Blue Strategies, a political fundraising and strategy firm, in 2008. By 2013, the firm had raised more than $4 million for political and public policy causes around North Carolina. She hired Broyhill to handle campaign finance reporting for Representative Brad Miller's campaign.

Jonathan spent so much time with the Hahns that some neighbors thought he lived with them. The three friends vacationed together and routinely had Monday night suppers together.

Jonathan felt comfortable enough with the Hahns to share with them that he was gay, not an easy topic for him in his small hometown and with his church upbringing. But he felt comfortable with the couple.

And he relied on them when he began to develop some serious health problems, particularly serious in a man only thirty-one years old. He shared with Jamie that he had multiple sclerosis. He stayed at their home to recuperate after gallbladder surgery, where the surgeon also found evidence of pancreatic cancer. The Hahns drove him to his follow-up appointment at Duke and waited in the lobby to take him home.

On April 22, 2013, Broyhill came to the Hahns' North Raleigh home for one of their regular Monday night dinners. A week before, Jamie had sent a text asking him about a $591 bounced check drawn on the campaign account and payable to Time Warner Cable. Tonight, Jamie wanted to clear up the issues.

She had tried several times to ask him about donors who said they hadn't received refunds after the Miller campaign was suspended and about the Federal Election Commission (FEC) quarterly report that hadn't been filed. Jonathan kept saying he'd been distracted by his medical issues but that he would take care of everything, not to worry. She knew he was dealing with a lot at the time. She trusted him. He'd taken care of things in the past. She'd been as patient as she could be, but she needed answers for the pressing questions her clients, the donors and the FEC were asking.

On Monday evening when Broyhill showed up for supper, Nation was upstairs changing clothes after going for a run. When he heard Jamie screaming, Nation raced down the stairs and saw her on the kitchen floor. Jonathan stood over her holding a knife.

Jamie fought hard against the frenzied attack, and Nation stepped in to shield her, suffering severe cuts to his fingers.

Nation yelled for Jamie to run. She made it out the door and to the neighbors' yard before she collapsed. In the 911 call logged at 5:19 p.m., the neighbor said, "She's bleeding so badly."

The neighbor tried to stanch the blood from the wounds on her abdomen until help arrived. Not knowing where Jamie had run from, first responders followed the trail of blood to her house.

Before EMTs arrived, Broyhill slit both of his wrists and stabbed himself in the stomach. The wound was so deep that responders reported his intestines were visible.

Jonathan later admitted he walked up behind Jamie and stabbed her in the back as she sat at the kitchen table. He'd purchased the large chef's knife a week earlier and brought it with him in his backpack.

The next day, as soon as Nation was released from WakeMed hospital with bandages on his wounds, he visited Jamie's bedside. Jamie died two days after the attacks, on April 24. She was twenty-nine years old.

Jonathan Broyhill recovered from his self-inflicted injuries and was released on April 30. He was charged with first-degree murder, attempted murder and assault with a deadly weapon with intent to kill inflicting serious injury. AWDWIKISI is the lengthy abbreviation for the only felony form of assault under North Carolina law; the *intent* to kill or to do serious injury separates it from other assault categories, which are classified as misdemeanors.

The Hahns' close friend Jonathan now faced serious charges, and investigators were trying to figure out what had happened.

The facts, as the layers peeled back, were stunning, attracting national and international attention: a friendship gone badly wrong, the compassionate nature of the victims, the behind-the-scenes glimpses of political fundraising and what turned out to be Broyhill's elaborate lies.

The Miller campaign account was missing at least $45,000. Broyhill was the employee who handled that account, the one with access to the campaign fundraising software.

Investigators also learned Jonathan had none of the illnesses he claimed to suffer. He didn't have MS and wasn't taking medication for it, he hadn't had gall bladder surgery and no doctor suggested he might have pancreatic cancer. When the Hahns drove him to Duke Cancer Center for his appointment and waited to take him home, Broyhill wandered around the hospital for two hours before returning to the lobby to announce that "he did indeed have pancreatic cancer, but the doctors were hopeful."

When Broyhill's trial started in February 2015, prosecutor Doug Faucette, in his opening statement, told the jury that Broyhill knew his "endless lies" were catching up with him and he came prepared to end the questions.

Broyhill's defense attorney argued that Broyhill suffered from depression and that he'd come to the Hahns' house because their home had been his refuge from pressures about his sexual orientation and his other struggles. He knew he couldn't answer Jamie's questions about the account, but he hadn't come to kill Jamie. He'd come to kill himself.

North Carolina Court of Appeals building in Raleigh. *Photo courtesy of the North Carolina Judicial Branch.*

The closing arguments in the case took more than three hours. The jury took less than an hour to return a verdict: guilty on all three charges. The judge sentenced Jonathan Broyhill to life in prison for murder, with consecutive terms of almost seventeen years for attempted murder and AWDWIKISI.

In 2017, the North Carolina Court of Appeals wrote what was a comparatively lengthy decision in a criminal appeals case. They dissected the defendant's arguments and found no error in the trial or the three custodial interrogations conducted while Broyhill was in the hospital. The court upheld the conviction.

The case attracted interest for several reasons but most notably for the character of the victims—an attractive, idealistic young couple who'd met and bonded over their passion for politics. They were out to change the world for the better and were working hard to make those passions a reality. Their compassion for others embraced their mutual friend Jonathan Broyhill, a man who apparently didn't have a lot of places to turn. They stood by him, and their friendship was repaid in an unimaginable act of violence.

Despite the tragic ending, the young couple's enthusiasm and warmth was the real heart of their story, the part that drew people to them and the part that endures.

8

SIDE TRIPS, CRIME BITS AND ODDITIES

Con Man on a Ledge

One might expect a man who made his living conning folks to have a flamboyant streak, and Daughn Arthur Cain did not disappoint.

In September 1951, the Wilson County Courthouse east of Raleigh hosted thirty-nine-year-old Cain's trial for forgery. Most small-town trials wouldn't attract attention from around the country, but then most small-town trials don't proceed while the defendant paces about on a ledge for two hours, seventy-five feet above the street, threatening to jump while the judge continues the trial inside.

Cain was charged with forging eleven checks, totaling $950 (roughly $9,775 today), from his employer, Littlejohn Faulkner. Faulkner, a former mayor of Wilson, owned a neon sign company. In the no-good-deed-goes-unpunished tradition, Faulkner had hired Cain on a conditional release from the Atlanta federal penitentiary, where he'd been serving time for forgery.

While being transferred from the jail to the courtroom for his trial, Cain slipped away from two officers and out onto the roof, where he dropped about eight feet down to the ledge.

The officers watching him were afraid he would either jump or fall. They described Cain as nervous.

In a town of about 23,000 people, the con man who stole from a former mayor managed to attract a crowd of 1,000 to 1,500 onlookers on the

Wilson County Courthouse, where Daughn Arthur Cain paced on the ledge during his 1951 trial. *Photo courtesy of the North Carolina Judicial Branch.*

courthouse grounds to watch him pace along the ledge. Some yelled for him to jump, called him "yellow." Officers on the roof above tried to get him to come inside.

As the early September morning grew warm, one reporter noted Cain pulled off his sports coat and draped it over his arm. As he paced along the four-foot ledge and the trial continued, Cain sometimes passed in view of the jury sitting in the courtroom.

A jail matron, whom Cain asked for, and a Catholic priest finally persuaded him he wouldn't be hurt if he got off the ledge and came inside.

Cain's defense attorney, obviously not a man to miss an opportunity, argued that his client didn't forge the eleven checks in question. Besides, he couldn't be guilty because he was clearly insane.

The jury spent eighty minutes of Cain's two-plus-hour sojourn deliberating in the jury room before finding him guilty.

Judge Henry L. Stevens Jr. minced no words. He told the jury, "I believe you reached a righteous conclusion. This was a man of superior intelligence and about the biggest flim-flam artist I've ever seen."

The judge also had words for Cain—after he was returned to the courtroom. "As for the performance you put on on the courthouse ledge, I certainly didn't believe for one minute that you'd jump, and I'm glad it turns out the jury didn't believe it either."

The judge immediately handed him a sentence up to ten years.

The story made headlines across the country, from Waynesville, North Carolina, to Louisville, Kentucky, to Spokane, Washington—often with an Associated Press wire photo of Cain holding onto a barred window while at least seven men tried to lower another man by rope onto the ledge. The story earned Cain a place in a 1984 *Charlotte Observer* round-up of Carolina con men—more for his flair for the dramatic than the size of his haul.

CRIME WRITER

In 1973, the entertainment editor for the *Raleigh News & Observer* introduced readers to a movie theater manager who loved both of his careers: showing movies and writing crime stories for the pulp magazines.

True crime magazines are now mostly wistful memories in these days of blogs and podcasts, but starting around 1920, the lurid covers of those magazines lined drugstore racks alongside true romance magazines—and often shared readership.

Starting in the 1940s, Cecil Winstead traveled the state writing for *Big-Book Detective*, *Master Detective* and the like—at the same time managing movie theaters around North Carolina.

Winstead said paychecks for writing, at three to five cents a word, were small and sometimes didn't cover expenses to travel or to buy photos—required by the publishers and furnished at the writer's expense. But he remembered every one of the ninety-one stories he'd published. His "stories from the police blotter" told tales from the Carolinas and elsewhere. His account of John Ashley and his early twentieth-century gang of Florida bootleggers and bank robbers was serialized on the *Gang Busters* radio show.

Two of the cases Winstead found that offered the mix of sex, violence and oddity the magazine readership expected involved, just by coincidence, gas stations.

In one, a thirty-nine-year-old Durham woman was found floating in Clearwater Lake near Chapel Hill in August 1955. Within a week, the Orange County sheriff arrested three teenagers—two who worked as gas station attendants, the third unemployed.

The woman had drowned, but her body showed bruising. The teens said they'd all had a "sex orgy" at the lake, but she was fine when they headed back to Durham at 2:00 a.m. She refused their offer of a ride.

Winstead apparently went a bit further afield, to Tennessee, for his other gas station case, this one involving voodoo. In 1947, Robert Waddy, paroled more than a decade earlier from a life sentence for murder, died in a shootout with police.

Waddy believed he'd been hexed by a voodoo spell. As a man who'd already been involved in two murders, he saw violence as a viable solution to his supernatural problem. First, he dynamited the gas station where the fortune-teller lived, injuring four people. The next day, he shot and wounded two women involved in hexing him.

For Winstead, managing movie theaters suited him because he liked movies. He also liked having his mornings free to write. The news photo shows him sitting behind his Underwood typewriter, a sheet of paper rolled in and ready for the next thrilling tale.

DURHAM CYCLE-GANG SHOOT-OUT

In July 1972, a panel truck traveling on I-85 north through Durham was blindsided with a barrage of gunfire. At least forty rounds hit the truck, killing two of the passengers and injuring three others. Only the driver escaped injury; he was arrested and charged with carrying a concealed weapon.

Inside the truck, police reported an inventory of weapons: six pistols, a rifle, a carbine, knives and ammunition.

The truck's passengers were members of the Miami chapter of the Pagans motorcycle club. They were traveling to their group's national headquarters in Washington, D.C., where the Pagans' original thirteen members first organized in 1964. By 1971, the group's national membership numbered in the hundreds, with thirty-seven chapters along the Eastern Seaboard.

At a Fort Lauderdale rally of various national clubs in January 1972, the Pagans must have met members of the Durham Storm Troopers club. The acquaintance they struck up apparently wasn't a happy one—some kerfuffle over stolen parts, maybe a motorcycle stolen at the gathering.

The Storm Troopers was a small regional cycle club—a much more civilized term than motorcycle gang—of fewer than twenty members. They were working on building their reputation—less than two years earlier, four members had been charged with fatally stabbing a man in a brawl outside a dance at Chapel Hill. All four were acquitted of that murder.

In July, someone tipped the Storm Troopers that the Pagans would be passing through Durham en route to Washington.

Someone else tipped the police about the identities of the Storm Troopers involved in the panel van shooting.

One of the Pagans' Washington members came to Durham to post bail for an injured member—the only female traveling in the truck. She had been arrested and held in Durham for slashing upholstery in a car. In an insult calculated to hit home, the Pagan from Washington said he'd never heard of the Storm Troopers, who, he said, were "just trying to make a name for themselves" by taking on the Pagans.

Motorcycle gang activity showed up on police blotters in the Triangle area, as it did over the rest of North Carolina in the 1970s. And, as with this case, unraveling what happened often required reading between the lines. Seldom did anyone offer to tell the whole story.

ODDITIES, NOT CRIMES

Balms for Broken Hearts

When former U.S. senator John Edwards's affair with a videographer he met during his 2008 presidential campaign came to light, his wife, Elizabeth, commented that she might consider a lawsuit against Andrew Young, her husband's former political aide who helped Edwards carry on his affair.

Some outside of North Carolina might have raised an eyebrow. Sue the person who admitted he helped hide an affair? That particular lawsuit was never filed, but North Carolina is one of a few remaining states that allow jilted spouses to sue for money damages, and such cases can be found in jurisdictions spread across the Tarheel State.

Case law from England, brought on sailing ships to America, consistently established the status of wives—effectively the same as servants. Neither wives nor servants could be lured away from their "masters" without the master having the right to assert his property rights against the one who did the luring. England abolished these actions in 1857.

These days, the specific terms for these cases—*criminal conversation* and *alienation of affection*—sound deliciously old-fashioned and a bit scandalous. Along with breach of promise to marry, these are known as "heart balm" actions because they aim to heal a broken heart.

Criminal conversation means, in short, a spouse (no sex discrimination here—again, it could be either the husband or the wife) has had sex with someone else and that someone must pay damages.

Alienation of affection is more complicated. Sex might have occurred but isn't required. And the lawsuit can be brought against anyone who helped alienate one spouse from the other—a lover, an in-law, a friend. Alienation cases require proof the couple was (1) "happily married and that a genuine love and affection existed," (2) "the love and affection was alienated and destroyed" and (3) the wrongful and malicious acts of the one being sued caused the alienation. That's the three-pronged test required to establish alienation of affection.

Often, the two types of cases are brought at the same time, because with criminal conversation and alienation of affection, one might lead to another.

While all this seems an odd throwback to a less enlightened time when women were considered property and a husband could demand repayment for lost property, these lawsuits are no joke. And today, they are decidedly equal opportunity—whether injured husband or wife, either may sue when affections have been stolen.

According to one count, as many as two hundred heart balm actions are filed in North Carolina every year. While it is not a crime to run around on your spouse, the resulting civil lawsuit can involve a great deal of money. Among those that go to trial, the dollar amounts awarded are staggering because remunerations frequently include punitive damages (damages designed to punish or make an example of the seducer). Awards mounting into millions of dollars are not uncommon.

One North Carolina case attracted international attention with the Lifetime movie *Broken Heart*. In 1997, Dorothy Hutelmyer sued her ex-husband's new wife in Alamance County. She alleged criminal conversation and all the elements of the three-pronged alienation test, stating in court filings that she and Mr. Hutelmyer enjoyed a "fairy-tale marriage," with their three children and their active community involvement, until her husband's secretary took to being "openly flirtatious."

A jury awarded her $1 million: $500,000 in actual damages and $500,000 in punitive damages.

The case sparked discussions in the state legislature and among the North Carolina bar about the need for repealing these antiquated laws. The Lifetime movie case wasn't the first to spark those discussions—and it wouldn't end the debate, either.

Other large-verdict cases were held as bench trials, decided by a judge only, rather than a perhaps easily swayed jury. In 2019, a man in Pitt County sued the man he claimed intentionally seduced his wife. The husband's attorney said the defendant laughed at the idea of such a lawsuit—but that was before the judge awarded $750,000 for the loss of the wife's affections. After the verdict, the attorney said, "That's a very dangerous perception to have because the same person who laughed at that deposition, that defendant now has a $750,000 judgment against them, so I don't think he's laughing now."

The same attorney who brought that case handled another record-setting case in 2010: $5.9 million awarded by a Pitt County judge, also in a non-jury trial.

An even larger verdict—$9 million—was awarded by a jury against a former dean at Guilford College who lured away another woman's lawyer-husband.

The following year, a Wake County judge ordered the new wife of a Raleigh trucking company owner to pay the ex-wife a record-setting $30 million—$10 million in actual damages, $20 million in punitive damages.

Of course, these verdicts are only paid if the person being sued has sufficient assets. Several family lawyers caution that headline-grabbing cases can air laundry that a couple's children and friends can find and read online even years later. In reporting on a 2018 verdict of $9 million in a Durham case, a *Washington Post* reporter noted the oddity of such awards, saying such cases, "in the modern era, mostly give rise to divorce and a lifelong grudge," rather than money damages. And the debate continues about whether these lawsuits are an insult and degradation to women by treating them as property or whether they are a viable legal reprisal for an injured spouse.

To date, only six other states continue to recognize this cause of action—Hawaii, Illinois, New Mexico, Mississippi, South Dakota and Utah. However, none of these states seem to indulge in these suits as lavishly as North Carolina does. As an interesting vestigial quirk of law, these cases remain among the state's legal oddities.

The Halloween *House*

Loving a horror movie is not a crime. Neither is loving a horror movie so much that you re-create the scary house and live in it. But it is odd enough to be noted.

The Myers House
North Carolina, Kenny
Caperton's tribute to
the movie *Halloween*.
Note: This is a private
residence. *Photo courtesy
of www.myershousenc.com.*

Kenny Caperton loved the 1978 John Carpenter movie *Halloween* so much that he wanted to immerse himself in it as much as physically possible. After visiting the original house in California, built in 1888, he decided to replicate it in North Carolina (as best he could while still making it livable—with a kitchen and bathrooms and modern appliances).

So, he re-created the Myers House, where "awful stuff happened there once," on a five-acre spread in Hillsborough. He moved in, along with memorabilia from the films, and often holds events around Halloween.

Please note the house isn't visible from the road and is a private residence. But visit his website (https://www.myershousenc.com/about) and check out opportunities to register for events at the house.

The Dream House

Another house, this one just a block off West Franklin Street in Chapel Hill, no longer exists, but it made headlines in 1992 when a reclusive old lady did battle with the university that had, over the decades, grown up around her dream home.

As a girl in Carrboro, Sallie Markham Hemphill Michie fell in love with the two-story white house with its deep porches at 121 South Columbia Street. With an inheritance left by her pharmacist father, she bought her dream house in 1919; she was in her early twenties at the time. She lived there until she died in 1992, at the age of ninety-six. She shared part of her life there with her second husband, a PhD student who failed to earn his degree. At other times, she took in boarders, most of them students at the university.

Above: A gargoyle guarding a campus building at UNC–Chapel Hill. *Photo by Cathy Pickens.*

Opposite: The Cryptozoology and Paranormal Museum in Littleton. Note: This is a museum and private residence. *Photo by Cathy Pickens.*

For the latter part of her life, she was lonely. In the early 1980s, she got in trouble for making unnecessary late-night calls to the police and fire departments, and the city tried to have her committed to an institution. The judge refused. She wasn't incompetent. As Walter Davis, one of her longtime friends, pointed out, "Judge, there is nothing wrong with that lady except that she lives in that big house and she's lonely."

Walter Davis first met Ms. Michie while reading meters for the university-owned electric company. Her meter was in her kitchen. Over time, as he saw how lonely and isolated she became, he took to visiting her most days and bringing her lunch on occasion. Even after he was promoted, he still read her meter and still looked after her in almost daily visits for twenty-five years.

Some felt she could be difficult. Some felt she hated the university. No matter the opinions about her personality or her sentiments, one thing was clear: she refused to leave her property to the University of North Carolina. Instead, she left it to the Daughters of the American Revolution (DAR) and the Magna Carta Dames, along with an endowment for its upkeep and the stipulation it should never be sold or leased.

Three years after her death, UNC won an eminent domain case declaring the property more valuable for public use by the university that now surrounded it than it was in the hands of two organizations that, frankly, didn't want to fight for it. The house was demolished, and the site hosted a temporary parking lot for more than a decade.

Cryptozoology and Paranormal House

The Research Triangle region also serves as home to a museum devoted to the study of creatures that many don't believe exist.

On its website, the International Cryptozoology Museum in Portland, Maine, claims it is the world's only such museum. The Cryptozoology and Paranormal Museum in Littleton, North Carolina, would beg to differ. Its website announced it was "dedicated to the study and display of creatures and phenomena not recognized by traditional science."

When Tony Barcelo, a former journalist with the *New York Daily News*, and his family relocated to Littleton, they found they'd bought a haunted house. Barcelo brought with him a fascination with Bigfoot, though he used to have to travel to upstate New York to pursue that interest. As he told reporter Alexandra Charitan, "We were lucky to see squirrels. There were no Bigfoot sightings on Long Island."

His haunted house and the area's Bigfoot sightings attract plenty of likeminded seekers to his house/museum, where he offers, among other treats, his expertise and a gift shop complete with a "Bigfoot go bag" with supplies for the do-it-yourself hunter. Check the website (https://crypto-para.org) for directions and times.

Scary movie houses where something awful *might* happen, parking lots that *should* be haunted because the house is gone and cryptids aren't crime scenes, but in a region noted for high-tech research and serious academic study, they're worth enjoying.

REFERENCES

Chapter 1

Mann/McBane

Associated Press. "N.C. Couple Killed by Lone Man—Doctor." *Charlotte Observer*, October 28, 1971.

Boyle, Louise. "Person of Interest Identified in Cold Case Murder of Young Couple Found Tortured in 'Lovers Lane' 42 Years Ago." *Daily Mail* (UK), November 15, 2013. https://www.dailymail.co.uk/news/article-2508062/Person-identified-42-year-old-cold-case-murder-young-couple.html.

Cutler, Amy. "Couple's Abduction, Torture, Murder Remains a Valentine's Day Mystery in Durham Almost 4 Decades Later." CBS 17, February 14, 2020. https://www.cbs17.com/news/local-news/durham-county-news/couples-abduction-torture-murder-remains-a-valentines-day-mystery-in-durham-almost-4-decades-later.

Krueger, Sarah. "DNA Collection Fails, but Podcast Pursues Clues in Orange County Cold Case." WRAL, June 14, 2018. https://www.wral.com/new-test-fails-to-find-enough-dna-to-close-orange-county-cold-case/17626847.

Pruitt, Eryk. "In the Long Dance, Two Journalists Reporting on a Cold Murder Case in Durham Become Podcasters Participating in an Investigation." *Indy Week*, July 4, 2018. https://indyweek.com/culture/

etc/long-dance-two-journalists-reporting-cold-murder-case-durham-become-podcasters-participating-investigation.

Pruitt, Eryk, and Drew Adamek. *The Long Dance*. 2018 and updates. Podcast, MP3 audio. https://thelongdancepodcast.com.

Warren-Hicks, Colin. "This Police Investigator Planned to Retire. But He Can't Let Go of a Cold Case in Durham." *Durham Herald-Sun*, July 5, 2018. https://www.heraldsun.com/news/local/crime/article213480714.html#storylink=cpy.

Faith Hedgepeth

Adams, Susan H., and Tracy Harpster. "911 Homicide Calls and Statement Analysis." *FBI Law Enforcement Bulletin*, June 2008, 22–31.

Blake, Suzanne. "Keeping Faith: Family and Police Grapple with Hedgepeth's Unsolved Murder Years Later." *Daily Tarheel*, September 6, 2019. https://www.dailytarheel.com/article/2019/09/faith-hedgepeth-anniversary-0906.

Blythe, Anne. "Court Documents Unsealed in Search for Faith Hedgepeth's Killer." *Raleigh News & Observer*, September 5, 2014. https://www.newsobserver.com/article10051073.html#storylink=cpy.

Cain, Brooke. "Seven Years After Faith Hedgepeth's Murder, a New Podcast Is Aimed at Generating Tips." *Raleigh News & Observer*, September 26, 2019 https://www.newsobserver.com/news/local/crime/article235458807.html#storylink=cpy.

Gasparoli, Tom. *Pursuit*. 2019. Podcast, MP3 audio. https://www.pursuitpodcast.com.

Jensen, Billy, and Paul Holes. "Who Killed Faith Hedgepeth?" *Jensen & Holes: The Murder Squad*. July 1, 2019. Podcast, MP3 audio. http://themurdersquad.com/episodes/who-killed-faith-hedgepeth. [Select evidence photos, Parabon phenotype sketch and audio recording of the 911 call available on this site.]

Taylor, John W. "The Murder of Faith Hedgepeth." *Crime Traveller*, June 3, 2019. https://www.crimetraveller.org/2017/09/death-of-faith-hedgepeth-getting-away-with-murder.

True Crime Daily (formerly *Crime Watch Daily*), series on Faith Hedgepeth case, 2016. https://truecrimedaily.com/search/?q=Faith+Hedgepeth.

Truesdell, Jeff. "8 Years After N.C. College Student's Murder, Mom Still Seeks Answers in Daughter's Death." *People*, May 28, 2020. https://people.com/crime/faith-hedgepeth.

Villenna, Cole. "Faith Hedgepeth: Things Hoped For, Things Unseen." *MediaHub*, December 8, 2017. http://mediahub.unc.edu/faith-hedgepeth-things-hoped-things-unseen.

"Who Killed the College Co-Ed: An ID Murder Mystery." *Investigation Discovery*, special report. May 28, 2020.

Wicker, Ann. "In Search of Susu." MFA thesis, Queens University of Charlotte, May 2005.

CHAPTER 2

Elusive DNA

"Drew Planten's Death Leaves Many Questions Unanswered." WRAL, updated May 8, 2008. https://www.wral.com/news/local/story/1091357.

"Calculated Coincidence." *Forensic Files*. Season 13, episode 14. Aired February 6, 2009.

"Catch Me If You Can." *Southern Fried Homicide*. Season 1, episode 5. Aired July 3, 2013.

Lamb, Amanda. *Evil Next Door: The Untold Story of a Killer Undone by DNA*. New York: Berkley, 2010.

"Vicious Voyeur." *Unusual Suspects*. Season 8, episode 4. Aired January 31, 2016.

Facebook Sleuths

Brown, Joel. "Meet the Nash County Woman Whose Facebook Page Helped Solve the Deborah Deans Case." ABC 11, October 26, 2019. https://abc11.com/kimberly-hancock-fighting-crime-facebook-page-cold-case/5648095.

Farberov, Snejana. "Tip Emailed to Administrator of 'Crime-Fighting' Facebook Page Leads Cops to the Buried Remains of a Murder Victim and the Arrest of Her Sister-in-Law in a 15-Year-Old Cold Case." *Daily Mail*, October 28, 2019. https://www.dailymail.co.uk/news/article-7622925/Tip-crime-fighting-Facebook-page-leads-womans-arrest-15-year-old-cold-case-murder.html.

Farzan, Antonia Noori. "She Was Charged with Murder 15 Years after Her Sister-in-Law Vanished. Police Credit a 'Crime Fighting' Facebook Page." *Washington Post*, October 28, 2019. https://www.washingtonpost.com/nation/2019/10/28/deborah-deans-cold-case-facebook-arrest-kimberly-hancock/.

Kay, Lindell J. "Murder Suspect Can Bail out of Jail." *Spring Hope Enterprise*, May 19, 2020. https://www.springhopeenterprise.com/stories/murder-suspect-makes-bail-in-sister-in-laws-killing,208184.

Owens, Adam. "Crime-Fighting Website Helped Crack Nash Cold Case Murder." WRAL, October 25, 2019. https://www.wral.com/crime-fighting-website-helped-crack-nash-cold-case-murder/18721677.

Rodriguez, Gloria, Joel Brown and Ana Rivera. "Woman Arrested for Murdering Sister-in-Law in 15-Year-Old Nash Co. Cold Case." ABC 11, October 25, 2019. https://abc11.com/remains-found-in-nash-co-could-belong-to-woman-missing-since-2004/5644352.

Genetic Genealogy

"Boy Under the Billboard: Frank Bender's Last Case." 6 ABC (Philadelphia), November 10, 2018. https://6abc.com/philadelphia-news-the-boy-under-billboard-frank-bender-forensic-bust/4654944.

Bridges, Virginia, and Tammy Grubb. "Man Charged with Killing 'Boy Under the Billboard' Pleads Guilty to Killing Son, Wife." WRAL, updated January 16, 2020. https://www.wral.com/father-in-court-21-years-after-boy-s-remains-found-under-mebane-billboard/18564914.

Capuzzo, Michael. *The Murder Room*. New York: Gotham, 2010.

Crump, Steve. "More Than 100+ Bodies Left Unidentified in North Carolina." WBTV (Charlotte), March 1, 2016.

Grubb, Tammy. "A Dogged Investigator Made Sure the 'Boy Under the Billboard' Was Not Forgotten." *Raleigh News & Observer*, February 5, 2019. www.newsobserver.com/news/local/article225508170.html#storylink=cpy.

Rowan, Tommy. "Filmmaker Releases Trailer for Documentary of Forensic Sculptor Frank Bender." *Philadelphia Inquirer*, May 28, 2015. https://www.inquirer.com/philly/news/Filmmaker_releases_trailer_for_documentary_of_forensic_sculptor_frank_bender.html.

CHAPTER 3

"*48 Hours Mystery*: A Killer Defense." CBS News, May 1, 2010. https://www.cbsnews.com/news/48-hours-mystery-a-killer-defense-01-05-2010.

Garret, Brandon L., and Peter J. Neufeld. *Invalid Forensic Science Testimony and Wrongful Convictions*, 95 Virginia L. Rev. 1 (2009).

Hewlett, Michael. "N.C. Supreme Court Allows Kirk Turner's Lawsuit against SBI Agents to Go Forward on Issue of Emotional Distress." *Winston-Salem Journal*, December 22, 2016. https://www.journalnow.com/news/crime/n-c-supreme-court-allows-kirk-turner-s-lawsuit-against/article_e8793ab2-940c-574f-9d66-bc76171238a4.html.

———. "SBI Settles with Clemmons Dentist Who Claimed Agents Tried to Frame Him for Wife's Killing." *Winston-Salem Journal*, April 27, 2018. https://www.journalnow.com/news/local/sbi-settles-with-clemmons-dentist-who-claimed-agents-tried-to-frame-him-for-wifes-killing/article_3f63261a-3368-5199-ad30-5b2c40cc12ed.html.

Hopper, Jessica. "Feds: North Carolina Crime Lab Buried Blood Evidence." ABC News, August 18, 2010. https://abcnews.go.com/WN.fbi-north-carolina-crime-law-buried-blood-evidence/story?id=11431980.

Hornshaw, Phil. "'The Staircase': Here's What Happened to Greg Taylor, the Man Exonerated After 17 Years in Prison." *The Wrap*, June 26, 2018. https://www.thewrap.com/the-staircase-greg-taylor-case.

Locke, Mandy, and Joseph Neff. "Agents' Secrets." *Raleigh News & Observer*, four-part series, August 10–13, 2010, updated April 7, 2015. https://www.newsobserver.com/news/special-reports/agents-secrets.

National Research Council of the National Academies. *Strengthening Forensic Science in the United States: A Path Forward*. Washington, D.C.: National Academies Press, 2009. http://nap.edu/12589.

Neff, Joseph. "Peterson Decision Squeezes Deaver." *Charlotte Observer*, December 18, 2011.

———. "SBI Expert's Partiality and Methods at Issue in Hearing." *Charlotte Observer*, December 8, 2011.

Neff, Joseph, and Mandy Locke. "Wrongly Jailed Men to Fet $12M." *Charlotte Observer*, August 13, 2013.

North Carolina v. Michael Peterson. Defendant's Motion for Appropriate Relief. Filed February 2011.

Peterson, Michael. *Behind the Staircase*. Privately published, January 2019.

PPSD Group. "Behind the Staircase: Exposing Jean-Xavier de Lestrade's Film." Accessed July 13, 2020. https://www.peterson-staircase.com/index.html.

Swecker, Chris, and Michael Wolf. *An Independent Review of the SBI Forensic Laboratory*, 2012. https://forensicresources.org/crime-labs.

Turner v. Thomas, 369 N.C. 419, 794 S.E.2d 439 (2016).

North Carolina Innocence Groups:

North Carolina Center on Actual Innocence. www.nccai.org.

North Carolina Innocence Inquiry Commission. www.innocencecommission-nc.gov.

CHAPTER 4

Arsenic Poisoning

Alibrandi, Tom, with Frank H. Armani. *Privileged Information*. New York: HarperCollins, 1984.

"Ann Miller Kontz." *Snapped*. Season 6, episode 21. July 6, 2008.

Arizona v. Macumber, 112 Ariz. 569, 544 P2d 1084 (1976).

Cain, Brooke. "Timeline: The Death of Eric Miller of Raleigh and the Murder Trial of His Wife Ann." *Raleigh News & Observer*, updated July 19, 2018. www.newsobserver.com/article215184005.html#storylink=cpy.

Lamb, Amanda. *Deadly Dose*. New York: Berkley, 2008.

———. "Kontz Avoids Life Sentence with Plea Deal in Husband's Death." WRAL, updated July 24, 2007. http://www.wral.com/news/local/story/121692/#Y0iBFs08v7Sqs8pS.99.

McKissock, Timothy M. "Where Ethical Rules and Morality Conflict." *South Carolina Lawyer*, July/August 1996, 15–17.

North Carolina Rules of Professional Conduct. www.ncbar.gov/rules/rules.asp.

"Toxic." *48 Hours*, CBS News. Aired March 14, 2009.

Trestrail, John. *Criminal Poisoning*. Totowa, NJ: Humana Press, 2000.

Weigl, Andrea. "Secrets May Not Ever Go to Jury." *Raleigh News & Observer*, June 13, 2004.

Whitmire, Tim. "Arsenic Endures as Stealthy Weapon." *Charlotte Observer*, February 10, 2001.

Insulin Poisoning

Heyndrickx A., Van Peteghem C., Van den Heede M., De Clerck F., Majelyne W. and Timperman J. "Insulin Murders: Isolation and Identification by Radio-Immunoassay after Several Months of Inhumation." In *Forensic Toxicology*, edited by Oliver J.S., 48–57. Boston: Springer, 1980.

Marks, Vincent, and Caroline Richmond. *Insulin Murders: True Life Cases*. London: Royal Society of Medicine Press, 2008.

Marks, Vincent. "Murder by Insulin: Suspected, Purported and Proven—A Review." *Drug Testing and Analysis*, April 1, 2009, 162–76.

"Murder Suspect Won't Face 3rd Trial." *Charlotte Observer*, January 9, 1992.

Quillin, Martha. "Gilmore Trial Ends in Second Deadlocked Jury." *Raleigh News & Observer*, October 19, 1989.

"2nd Insulin Trial Deadlocks." *Charlotte Observer*, October 10, 1989.

State v. Gilmore, 330 NC 167, 409 SE2d 888 (1991).

CHAPTER 5

Joan Little

Acker, James R. "The Trial of Joan Little: An Inmate, a Jailer, and a First-Degree Murder Charge." In *Famous American Crimes and Trials*. Vol. 4, edited by Frankie Y. Bailey and Steven Chermak, 193–209. Westport, CT: Praeger, 2004.

Greene, Christina. "She Ain't No Rosa Parks." *Journal of African-American History* 100, no. 3 (Summer 2015): 428–47.

Reston, James Jr. Collection of Joan Little Trial Materials, 1975–6. Collection Number 04006, UNC University Libraries (including trial testimony, audio interviews and news reports). https://finding-aids.lib.unc.edu/04006/.

———. "The Joan Little Case." *The New York Times Magazine*, April 6, 1975. https://www.nytimes.com/1975/04/06/archives/the-joan-little-case-in-a-small-southern-town-the-night-jailer-is.html.

———. *The Innocence of Joan Little: A Southern Mystery*. New York: Times Books, 1977.

Reston, James Jr., Joan Little and Mark Pinsky. "Who Is Joan Little?" *Southern Exposure* 6, no. 1 (1978).

Spy in Hiding

Elliston, Jon. "After the Molehunts." *Indy Week*, September 3, 2003. https://indyweek.com/news/archives/molehunts.

————. "Spy Like Us?" *Indy Week*, March 7, 2001. https://indyweek.com/news/archives/spy-like-us.

Patterson, Donald W. "Diplomat Falls Hard, Lands in Chapel Hill; in N.C., He Bagged Groceries." *Greensboro News & Record*, January 16, 1993. https://www.greensboro.com/diplomat-falls-hard-lands-in-chapel-hill-in-n-c/article_da3cf81c-4f67-5184-b81d-5ff94883a5b5.html.

Wise, David. "The Felix Bloch Affair." *The New York Times Magazine*, May 13, 1990.

————. *Spy: The Inside Story of How the FBI's Robert Hanssen Betrayed America.* New York: Random House (2002).

Prison Break

Charlotte Observer, December 9, 1959.

Schlosser, Jim. "Ex-Con Recalls His Great Escapes." *Greensboro News & Record*, September 25, 1993. https://www.greensboro.com/ex-con-recalls-his-great-escapes/article_e4723153-cf02-55fc-b31d-83d540adc559.html.

Shaffer, Josh. "NC's 'Little Alcatraz,' Famous Jailbreak Prison, Is for Sale." *Raleigh News & Observer*, January 13, 2017. https://www.newsobserver.com/article126361489.html#storylink=cpy.

Steelman, Ben. "Celebrated Trooper Swartz Dies at 85." *Wilmington Star-News*, September 13, 2012.

Chapter 6

Dungeons & Dragons

Baird, Scott. "15 Controversies That Almost Destroyed Dungeons & Dragons." *Screen Rant*, January 21, 2018. https://screenrant.com/dungeons-and-dragons-controversies-almost-destroyed-game.

Bledsoe, Jerry. *Blood Games*. New York: Dutton, 1991.

Busch, Frederick. "Crime/Mystery: The Blood on the Bedroom Ceiling." *The New York Times*, October 20, 1991. https://www.nytimes.com/1991/10/20/books/crime-mystery-the-blood-on-the-bedroom-ceiling.html.

Cain, Brooke. "All in the Family: Notorious NC Murders That Struck Close to Home." *Raleigh News & Observer*, December 7, 2018. https://www.newsobserver.com/news/local/article222789440.html#storylink=cpy.

Clement, Hayes. "Son Wanted Inheritance; Students Act Out Fantasy Game Scenario in Real-Life Murder." *Greensboro News & Record*, January 27, 1990. https://www.greensboro.com/son-wanted-inheritance-students-act-out-fantasy-game-scenario-in/article_4bbf18c4-e2af-5736-b37d-57514a255900.html.

Gilsdorf, Ethan. "A Game as Literary Tutorial." *The New York Times*, July 14, 2014.

"The Great 1980s Dungeons & Dragons Panic." *BBC News Magazine*, April 11, 2014. https://www.bbc.com/news/magazine-26328105.

McGinniss, Joe. *Cruel Doubt*. New York: Simon & Schuster, 1991.

The New York Times News Service. "Murder, He Wrote—Repeatedly." *Baltimore Sun*, October 2, 1991.

Rowe, Jeri. "A Story He Couldn't Pass Up; In Race to Write, Author Soaked up Sights, Smell of Murder Case." *Greensboro News & Record*, August 17, 1991. https://www.greensboro.com/a-story-he-couldn-t-pass-up-in-race-to/article_80029269-22b5-537e-bb81-5a97d212c3a4.html.

State v. Upchurch, 332 N.C. 439, 421 S.E.2d 577 (1992).

Innocence or Guilt

Associated Press. "False Confession Expert Testifies in NC Innocence Case." WCTI12 News, August 21, 2019. https://wcti12.com/news/state-news/false-confession-expert-testifies-in-nc-innocence-case.

DeGrave, Sam. "Support Group Forms for Families of Buncombe Murder Victims." *Asheville Citizen-Times*, April 23, 2018. https://apnews.com/65f5183c95034f0d8a8ace599ab198f6.

Lamb, Amanda. "Convicted Killer Paroled After Decades in Prison for NC State Student's Death." WRAL, May 27, 2019. https://www.wral.com/convicted-killer-paroled-released-after-decades-in-prison-for-nc-state-student-s-death/18414553.

North Carolina Center on Actual Innocence. https://www.nccai.org.

North Carolina Innocence Inquiry Commission. https://www.innocencecommission-nc.gov.

Parks, Jean. "Opinion: Another View on Closure on Murder Cases." *Asheville Citizen-Times,* January 30, 2015. https://www.citizen-times.com/story/opinion/contributors/2015/01/30/another-view-closure-murder-cases/22599601/.

Shaffer, Josh. "'I Never Did Hate You,' Sister of Murdered NC State Student Tells Convicted Killer." *Raleigh News & Observer,* September 11, 2019. https://www.newsobserver.com/news/local/article234734732.html#storylink=cpy.

State v. Blackman [*sic*], 377 S.E.2d 290 (1989).

State v. Goldman, 317 S.E.2d 361 (1984).

Waggoner, Martha. "North Carolina Man Exonerated by Panel in 1979 Dorm Slaying." *US News & World Report*, August 22, 2019. https://www.usnews.com/news/best-states/north-carolina/articles/2019-08-22/judges-begin-deliberating-innocence-of-1979-murder-convict.

Chapter 7

Robert Petrick

CRN Staff. "'Google Murder' Trial Nearing Conclusion." CRN, November 30, 2005. https://www.crn.com/news/channel-programs/174402848/google-murder-trial-nearing-conclusion.htm.

Glass, Nancy, et al. "Non-Fatal Strangulation Is an Important Risk Factor for Homicide of Women." *Journal of Emergency Medicine* 35, no 3 (October 2008): 329–35. https://www.ncbi.nlm.nih.gov/pmc/articles/PMC2573025.

Kotb, Hoda. "Facing the Music." NBC *Dateline*, July 15, 2007. http://www.nbcnews.com/id/13121431/ns/dateline_nbc/t/facing-music/#.Xrqvoi-ZOb-.

Pérez-Peña, Richard. "Why Do Killers Represent Themselves? Ego, Ideology, Paranoia." *The New York Times*, January 5, 2017. https://www.nytimes.com/2017/01/05/us/dylann-roof-killers-defense-lawyers.html.

Petrick v. Thornton, Memorandum Opinion & Order, U.S. Federal District Court Middle District of North Carolina, November 21, 2014. https://www.govinfo.gov/content/pkg/USCOURTS-ncmd-1_09-cv-00551/pdf/USCOURTS-ncmd-1_09-cv-00551-1.pdf.

State v. Petrick, 186 N.C. App. 597, 652 S.E.2d 688 (November 6, 2007).

WRAL coverage of the case, https://www.wral.com/news/local/asset_gallery/1087192/.

Mail Bomb

"Bombing Incidents Known to Police." *Sourcebook of Criminal Justice Statistics 2003*, 337. https://nicic.gov/sourcebook-criminal-justice-statistics-0.

Dill, Stephen. "Man Found Guilty in Bombing; Bullis Expected to Get Life Term." *Charlotte Observer*, February 15, 1996.

Jarvis, Craig, and Mark Stencel. "Victim's Husband Charged in Blast." *Raleigh News & Observer*, July 16, 1995.

McFadden, Kay, and Foon Rhee. "Bomb Explodes in Raleigh." *Charlotte Observer*, July 11, 1995.

Wiehl, Lis, with Lisa Pulitzer. *Hunting the Unabomber*. Nashville: Thomas Nelson, 2020.

Political Connections

"Best Man 'Who Stabbed Couple, Killing Wife, Had Been Faking Cancer During Investigation into Thousands of Dollars Missing from Victim's Company.'" *Daily Mail*, April 26, 2013. https://www.dailymail.co.uk/news/article-2315275/Jonathan-Broyhill-Best-man-stabbed-couple-faking-cancer-investigation-missing-finances.html.

Blythe, Anne. "Defense Says Jonathan Broyhill Only Planned to Kill Himself, Not Jamie Hahn." *Charlotte Observer*, March 4, 2015. https://www.charlotteobserver.com/news/local/article12544787.html#storylink=cpy.

———. "Man Convicted of Killing Democratic Strategist Jamie Hahn Won't Get New Trial." *Raleigh News & Observer*, July 18, 2017. https://www.newsobserver.com/news/local/crime/article162229448.html#storylink=cpy.

"Police Officer Says Raleigh Murder Scene Was Worst He's Seen in 10-Year Career." ABC 11, March 6, 2015. https://abc11.com/news/officer-says-raleigh-murder-scene-was-worst-hes-seen/547354.

State v. Jonathan Wayne Broyhill, 803 S.E.2d 832 (N.C. Ct. App. 2017). https://caselaw.findlaw.com/nc-court-of-appeals/1868112.html.

Chapter 8

Con Man

"Carolina Con Men." *Charlotte Observer*, April 1, 1984.

"Defendant Stands Trial on Ledge of Courthouse; Found Guilty Despite Threats to Jump." *Charlotte Observer*, September 7, 1951.

"Man Teeters on Ledge As His Trial Goes On." *Louisville Courier-Journal*, September 7, 1951.

Crime Writer

"'Hexed' Negro Slain in Duel." *Charlotte Observer*, July 5, 1947.

Morrison, Bill. "Tracking Crime and Cinema Through Carolina Country." *Raleigh News & Observer*, November 4, 1973.

"Three Youths Are Charged with Murder." *Charlotte Observer*, September 2, 1955.

Gang Shoot-Out

Alridge, Ron, and Peggy Payne. "Grudge Led to Shoot-Out." *Charlotte Observer*, July 2, 1972.

Observer Wire and Staff Reports. "4 Charged in Fatal Stabbing." *Charlotte Observer*, November 22, 1970.

Heart Balm

Anderson, Ann. "Court of Appeals Holds That 'Heart Balm' Claims Are Not Facially Unconstitutional." *UNC School of Government* (blog), September 6, 2017. https://civil.sog.unc.edu/court-of-appeals-holds-that-heart-balm-claims-are-not-facially-unconstitutional.

Fowler, Hayley. "NC Man Wins $750,000 from Former Wife's Lover." *Charlotte Observer*, October 6, 2019.

Gomstyn, Alice, and Lee Ferran. "Wife's $9M Message to Mistresses: 'Lay Off'." *Good Morning America*, March 19, 2020. https://abcnews.go.com/GMA/Business/wife-wins-million-husbands-alleged-mistress/story?id=10177637.

Leonard, James. "*Cannon v. Miller*: The Brief Death of Alienation of Affections and Criminal Conversation in North Carolina." 63 North Carolina Law Review 1317 (1985). http://scholarship.law.unc.edu/nclr/vol63/iss6/26.

Ravenelle, Alexandrea. "Movie Based on Alamance Adultery Lawsuit: An Alamance Alienation of Affection Case Is Retold in a Television Movie." *Greensboro News & Record*, August 12, 1999. https://www.greensboro.com/movie-based-on-alamance-adultery-lawsuit-an-alamance-alienation-of-affection-case-is-retold-in/article_a3f02592-ca71-557c-a936-b05fe3f7c4c1.html.

Stanley-Becker, Isaac. "$8.8 million 'Alienation of Affection' Penalty: Another Reason Not to Have an Affair." *Washington Post*, July 31, 2018. https://www.washingtonpost.com/news/morning-mix/wp/2018/07/31/8-8-million-alienation-of-affection-award-another-reason-not-to-have-an-affair-in-north-carolina.

The Halloween *House*

Myers House, Hillsborough, NC. https://www.myershousenc.com/about.

The Dream House

Grubb, Tammy. "Can Eminent Domain Save the Colonial Inn?" *Raleigh News & Observer*, August 15, 2014. https://www.newsobserver.com/news/local/community/chapel-hill-news/article10032956.html#storylink=cpy.

Perlmutt, David. "From Grave, She Still Fights UNC's Plans for Her House." *Charlotte Observer*, December 26, 1992.

Cryptozoology and Paranormal House

Charitan, Alexandra. "Bigfoot in Littleton: Meet the Former NYC Journalist Who Turned His Haunted House into a Cryptozoology and Paranormal Museum." *Roadtrippers Magazine*, October 22, 2019. https://roadtrippers.com/magazine/crypto-para-museum-littleton.

Cryptozoology and Paranormal Museum, Littleton, NC. https://crypto-para.org.

ABOUT THE AUTHOR

Cathy Pickens, a lawyer and college professor, is a crime fiction writer (*Southern Fried Mysteries*, St. Martin's/Minotaur) and true crime columnist for *Mystery Readers Journal*. She is professor emerita in the McColl School of Business and served as national president of Sisters in Crime and on the boards of Mystery Writers of America and the Mecklenburg Forensic Medicine Program (an evidence collection/preservation training collaborative).

She is also the author of *CREATE!* (ICSC Press), offers coaching and workshops on developing the creative process and works with writers on telling their stories. Her other books from The History Press include *Charlotte True Crime Stories*, *True Crime Stories of Eastern North Carolina* and *Charleston Mysteries*.